NN 10/19			

This item is to be returned or renewed before the latest date above. It may be borrowed for a further period if not in demand. **To renew your books:**

- **Phone the 24/7 Renewal Line 01926 499273 or**
- **Visit www.warwickshire.gov.uk/libraries**

  Discover ● Imagine● Learn ● *with libraries*

Warwickshire
County Council

Working for Warwickshire

D0239270

Three Circles into One

William Waldegrave

Mensch Publishing

Mensch Publishing
51 Northchurch Road, London N1 4EE, United Kingdom

First published in Great Britain 2019

ISBN: PB: 978-1-912914-10-4;
eBook: 978-1-912914-11-1

Typeset by Van-garde Imagery, Inc., Florida, United States

To my children
Katie, Liza, Jamie and Harriet
Whose generation will have to pick up the pieces

Contents

Foreword ix

Chapter One: This Feels Different 1

Chapter Two: The First Two Circles 7

Chapter Three: The Third Circle 17

Chapter Four: Is it Really About Europe at All? . . . 27

Chapter Five: Collateral Damage 35

Chapter Six: Systemic Damage 49

Chapter Seven: Can Normal Service Be Resumed? . . 61

Chapter Eight: Stores, Bad and Magical 67

Chapter Nine: Singapore-On-Thames 83

Chapter Ten: The USAGBNI? 93

Chapter Eleven: The Return 97

Chapter Twelve: Punching at our Correct Weight . . 107

Chapter Thirteen: Envoi 121

About the Author 125

Foreword

As I WRITE IN the warm summer of 2019, Britain is moving, fast, towards a political and more than political crisis which feels quite different from anything, I at least, have experienced before. Old party allegiances are crumbling as we watch and the Kingdom is at very real risk of dissolution, with the claim that Boris Johnson may be the last Prime Minister of the United Kingdom of Great Britain and Northern Ireland not quite absurd. Large swathes of industry face what some of its leaders describe as 'Armageddon' and Parliament seems incapable of doing its job of mediating our conflicts and finding a way forward. Anger and bitterness divide us. The world watches as what was once taken to be the most skilful democracy in the world rattles toward what looks like a chaotic crash.

How on earth did we get here, after what at least on

the surface looked like a very long period of broadly consistent and successful leadership? What happens next?

I will argue that the referendum result which led us to wake up in a different country on that June morning in 2016 had roots which lay in the slow dissolution of the national narrative of our identity, which was crafted after the Second World War. I do not believe in inexorable processes of history, and things could have been different if different decisions had been taken by different personalities – but the waves through which leaders have to steer have their origins.

This short book is not a doomed attempt to predict exactly what will happen in the next six months or the next year or two. It is impossible, however, to attempt the second half of my essay – namely a sketch of what narratives Britain might adopt in the future to replace the one which is lost – without considering, as everyone else in the country is considering, the difficulties immediately ahead. I describe the Brexit process, whether completed or frustrated, as a toxic and sulphurous ditch. And cross it we have to: history may not be driven by inexorable forces, but it does not stop.

Then, whatever has happened, a massive task of national reconstruction will need to be undertaken. What will need rebuilding will be the damaged institutions, damaged allegiances to those institutions and damaged mutual trust among citizens. My thesis is that none of this necessary rebuilding will be achievable unless we settle on a new and coherent national narrative to replace that which has now dissolved. What kind of a country will we want to be? In my consideration of four possible future national narratives, I must make some guesses at what could happen on the way across the Brexit ditch, in order to show why I think the damage we have already inflicted upon ourselves will get much worse, and will not allow for any easy return to a lost normality.

Let me be clear about one thing: I believe that Britain can live sensibly outside the European Union just as it can live sensibly within it. What is toxic, however, is the political process which started with the referendum campaign and has continued ever since. This process is far from finished and its toxicity will be likely to increase before it is completed. Its exact course is difficult to predict but the damage it has done, is doing, and will continue to do for some time yet, is all too easy to see.

I do not believe the worth of my analysis depends on the accuracy of my predictions for the immediate future. All I argue is that the next period of our islands' story will not be plain sailing. If I am wrong in that, well, let us sing Hallelujah.

1   This Feels Different

DOES THIS NOT FEEL different? Since I was born in 1946, political crises have come and gone, but they came and went as episodes in a continuing story – the continuation of which we did not doubt. Some chapters were disastrous: a mad government lied to us over the invasion of Egypt in the Suez Crisis of 1956, involving us in a doomed and secret conspiracy with the French and Israeli governments. There was bitter recrimination within the political classes when the venture failed. Families argued and dissenting members of Parliament were deselected in the name of a patriotism stirred up by a disreputable nationalistic popular press. However, within two years the government which had conducted the fiasco (after little more self-analysis than a change of leader), was re-elected with a much larger majority than before, and very nearly won the next election after that into the bargain.

Most of the national story went on its way. We shed empire largely peaceably, modernised social attitudes, become more prosperous, chose governments sometimes of the centre-left and sometimes of the centre-right. Taxation sometimes went up and sometimes went down. Anxieties – mostly ill-founded – about our relative failure compared to other nations industrially or economically led to changing fashions in policies. Sometimes French statism was the latest thing; sometimes Scandinavian or West German consensus-based soft corporatism; for a while American business school efficiency ruled the roost, then came a dose of free market liberalism. Things went on. A 2 to 2 ½ per cent long-term growth rate was not much different from that of any other mature economy, once those which had been laid waste by the Second World War had rebuilt themselves at speed and settled down to maturity once again.

A hard chapter was the restoration of powers to Parliament challenged by organised labour: bitter industrial conflict in the seventies and eighties, some of it with a genuine revolutionary tinge on the part of some union leaders, did indeed induce a different kind of crisis, and took courage and determination to defeat. The defeat was enabled by social democrats in the unions and the political parties as much as by Conservatives in parliament. The solution of this conflict strengthened, rather than weakened, the parliamentary and broader political institutions which carried the country through.

At some times, pessimism and even defeatism infected our rulers. There were strange (and in retrospect, comic) fantasies at over-lubricated dinner parties: would Lord Mountbatten, assisted by an implausible newspaper magnate called Cecil King, take the country over to rescue us from our ungovernability and flush out the reds from under the bed? No, he would not. There was no revolution or counter-revolution. There were deeply held divisions of opinion, leading to civil disobedience and mass protest from time to time. But, for example, large ban-the-bomb marches to Aldermaston, where Britain makes nuclear weapons, passed off peaceably, led by the aristocratic logician and philosopher Bertrand Russell, who had once proposed the pre-emptive atomic bombing of the Soviet Union but had changed his position.

If you recognised as a youngster of my generation the smell of tear gas, it was because of visits to Paris, Athens, or even, on occasion, Cambridge, Massachusetts. Not from walking down a Whitehall which still maintained a public right of way through Downing Street and under the Cabinet Office onto Horse Guards Parade, guarded by unarmed policemen.

So the story seemed to continue. We British, we told ourselves, were the world's most skilful players of the game of politics, at home and abroad. Our socialists were patriotic. They stood up to Stalinism, built the National Health Service, and facilitated the necessary shifts in social policy at home. Our conservatives abhorred nationalist rhetoric, deployed Keynesian economics, accepted that if things were to stay the same they had to change and relinquished empire, suppressing the nostalgic imperialism of their older supporters. The two groups fought over whether the state should control 40 per cent of the national wealth or 60 per cent, and the nation usually ended up somewhere in between.

All this was mediated by institutions which though often ridiculed, were deeply trusted. Parliament above all, which possessed enormous powers vested in those who controlled it, did not abuse those powers. They were limited by conventions that were respected and by the electoral success which seemed to derive from rather moderate promising at election time. The civil service and the armed forces were apolitical, serving the Queen – a constitutional concept physically embodied with miraculous grace in the person of Elizabeth II. The judiciary, the scientists, the health service and the BBC – all these were the institutions, or the lineal descendants of the institutions, which had brought us honourable victory in 1945.

No other significant country in Europe could say

the same: not Germany, not France, not Italy, not Spain. Of course we mocked our beloved institutions. That was one of our ancient liberties! We did not, however, much care for others mocking them. We thought we had the right to trust them. We had no Lenin, Stalin, Hitler, Pétain, Mussolini or Franco for whom to apologise, or to defend with lies. Our moderation and restraint gave us George Orwell as a hero, implacably even-handed in his denunciation of the identical extremism of right and left, and of imperialism old and new. It gave us P.G. Wodehouse equipping us to laugh the preposterous Oswald Mosley out of court in the guise of Sir Roderick Spode.

Our philosophy was to have no philosophy. When the right felt the need to decorate its speeches with quotations from books of the past, they were the books of careful empiricists such as David Hume and Adam Smith, from the eighteenth-century enlightenment or the romantic novels of Disraeli, the former the great texts of scepticism and caution, the latter the source of engaging fantasy. The left were students of sixteenth-century parliamentarianism (minus the religious fundamentalism), of the mystical William Blake, and of William Morris's respect for the value of the craftsman much more than of Marx's Hegelian historicism or his pernicious conspiracy theories.

2 The First Two Circles

OF COURSE, BRITAIN BETWEEN 1945 and today was no idyll, nor was there any golden age before that. There were sometimes bitter battles, political and social. There was injustice and failure in Ireland in the nineteenth century and then in Northern Ireland, in the declining Victorian industrial areas and in too-long delayed social reforms. However, the failures were not systemic: good people working our institutions, most believed, could make things better – and those who believed that any other system, communist or fascist, corporatist or anarchist, could make them perfect, found few adherents. Our national character, embodied in our institutions, would see us through to an acceptable future.

There was a national community, governable by consensus even at times of bitter dispute. The structures of civil society were multifarious and deep-rooted. As a national family we could quarrel bitterly, but we were family. Even radical critics accepted the metaphor: Orwell wrote that we were a family, but with the wrong members in charge. The strength of this domestic allegiance to our institutions served us exceptionally well in by far the greatest and most dangerous historical transition we had to make. What is most remarkable about Britain's history since 1945 is not that we faced the normal domestic problems of an advanced economy in a changing social and technological world with some skill and success. Other nations did that, sometimes with greater skill than we. The extraordinary achievement – so large an elephant in the room that many commentators miss it altogether – is the scale of the change in our overseas global position, and how easily this titanic process passed in one swift generation.

It is hard to think of any other tremendous imperial power, in recent times or earlier, which passed through such a transition so smoothly. This relatively calm acceptance of an extraordinarily rapid change in Britain's position in the world is in retrospect astonishing. The overwhelming national identity, as late as the period between the first and second world wars, was still imperial. Empire Day meant something to millions; our navy still claimed to be the greatest in the world, and we sang about it without irony. His supporters praised the dreadful General Dyer, responsible for the massacre at Amritsar in 1919, for having 'saved India'. Churchill told us in 1940 that the finest hour then at hand was that of a British Empire and Commonwealth which might last a thousand years. When the term 'superpower' became fashionable after 1945, coined by American foreign policy professor William T. R. Fox, it was applied to three powers: the United States, the USSR and the British Empire.

Within twenty years all this had almost entirely gone from our national narrative, without the horrors of the wars France fought in Indochina and Algeria and the near civil war she subsequently faced at home; without that imperial role having been taken from us by defeat like Germany and Italy and Japan, and without the chaos and still unresolved resentment we witnessed later at the dissolution of the Soviet Empire. It was the result not of chance but of conscious political leadership and the invention and popularisation of a new national narrative designed to replace the old imperialism, just close enough to the truth to work, but a beneficial fiction nonetheless. This was the doctrine of British exceptionalism embodied in the Three Circles.

The story of the Three Circles did not invent itself. It was crafted quite consciously by some of the greatest masters of political rhetoric of modern times. It was first set out in characteristic style by the greatest of them all,

Winston Churchill, in a speech to Welsh Conservatives at Llandudno in October 1948. He described a Britain uniquely placed at the centre of 'three majestic circles': Empire, the English-Speaking World (really America) and Europe. The empire had been transmuted by wise and benevolent leadership into a Commonwealth of Nations, with the Queen at its head. The Second Circle was our Special Relationship with the United States, allegedly forged in the heat of the Second World War, one which could not be matched by any other European ally. The Third Circle was Europe, our geographic home, rebuilding itself after the war. Churchill was equivocal about our relationship with this renascent Europe – the imperialism bred in his bones naturally led him to assume the primacy of the old imperial connections. But he knew we could not ignore Europe.

Finally, Harold Macmillan, the political magician who steered us so skilfully to the voluntary dissolution of our remaining colonies, concluded that for our effective participation in the Third Circle, geography was not enough: we had actually to seek membership of the nascent European political enterprise started by France and Germany and encouraged by Churchill. So, Macmillan led us to seek membership of the European Economic Communities.

Winds of Change written by Peter Hennessy, the doyen of contemporary historians, gives a brilliant account of Macmillan's conscious planning for Britain's new place in the world and of the analysis – undertaken by himself, not by think tanks or special advisers – which lay behind it. Hennessy's chapter is quite properly headed 'Grand Design' – and so it was; a reminder of a time when a prime minister had the experience and intellectual capacity himself to create a successful strategy for the nation, a strategy which has served us well for nearly sixty years.

Thus was consciously designed our New Elizabethan role, invented at the very moment when American diplomat Dean Acheson analysed our plight as a nation that had lost an empire and not yet found a role. From that year, 1962, onwards our narrative became that of the wise and stable polity uniquely at the centre of the three overlapping Venn diagram circles of the free world: the Commonwealth, the US, and non-communist Europe.

This was an enormous achievement of political leadership, enabling enough of the British people to accept a new position in the world with dignity and pride. It was another kind of victory, once again delivered by our ancient institutions, and derived from the pragmatic, non-doctrinaire liberalism which underlay the doctrines of our main political parties. It reinforced both the institutions and the pragmatic philosophy which imbued them.

All of our institutions evolved at home and abroad to provide the underpinning structures of a new national narrative. Our defence and intelligence strategy was constructed around the American led North Atlantic Treaty Organisation. Our Commonwealth, no longer just British, but with the Queen universally accepted as its head, added the 'C' to the initials of the old FO which became the FCO. And when, finally, we circumnavigated the French veto and joined the institutions of what is now the EU in 1971, our constitution adapted itself to the acceptance of law passed in Brussels and adjudicated in Strasbourg, while our industry and commerce integrated itself with the greatest common market and customs union in the world. We passed from superpower to a new role as a crucial lynch pin, or so our national narrative told us, of the structure of the civilised world.

Skilfully though it may have been done, each element of the new narrative brought its dangers and bred mostly subterranean tension. Take the Commonwealth circle. The empire had (largely) fought for us in the war – did its citizens not have the right to come to the mother country, citizens of a universal empire as St Paul had once been of the Roman? Initially, St Paul's demand that as a Roman citizen he had the right to go to Rome for justice found an echo in an imperial 'civis Britannicus sum'. Our imperial brethren and sisters surely had the right to come to the mother country for which in many cases they had loyally fought.

In search of labour to rebuild a war-damaged Britain and its industries after 1945, we invited immigration from our empire, from the West Indies, from India and Pakistan and Africa. Labour Prime Minister Clement Attlee on one occasion asked his colonial secretary if he could not raise an imperial army of a million men from Africa (John Bew, *Citizen Clem*, p. 423) to replace the Indian army we were losing, and which had made us for the only time in our history a first-rank power on land as well as on the sea. More realistically, Tories invited West Indians to fill jobs in the Health Service and Punjabis to help man the textile and transport industries. Forgetfulness of this warmly invited *Empire Windrush* generation has recently disgraced the Home Office. There was also traffic the opposite way: Second World War ex-servicemen were given support to settle in Kenya or Southern Rhodesia, which is now Zimbabwe.

We were perhaps a little optimistic about the ease with which old prejudices would die away. The British were not and are not magically immune to racial prejudice, which is a universal human failing rooted far back in antique tribalism. There were plenty in the communities which saw rapid change of racial mix at the same time as the decline of traditional jobs, who thought the one had caused the other. Others felt betrayed by the arrival of new competitors for such jobs as there were, or were simply angered by the arrival of neighbours with different traditions, skin colour and habits than their own. Those who felt like this did not much love the concept of an inclusive Commonwealth.

Or consider the 'Special Relationship'. The Suez debacle had shown those willing to think clearly that even alongside an ally as significant as France, Britain did not have the freedom of action it would formerly have taken for granted. Once, it would have been axiomatic that the two principal military powers in Europe, both members of the UN Security Council, could take military action to protect what they regarded as important economic and strategic interests without US permission. By 1956, not so.

Indeed, as Andrew Roberts shows in his book *Masters and Commanders*, there was never any pretence of equality in the wartime relationship between the US and the UK – at least after the Casablanca conference of 1943. An excellent account of the ruthlessness of post-war US policy in relation to Britain is shown in Richard Davenport Hines's *Universal Man: The Seven Lives of John Maynard Keynes*. The book describes Keynes's attempt in Washington in the year leading up to his premature death in 1946, to alleviate some of the economic burden laid on their ally by America's wartime loans. As Orwell noticed, part of the American assumption during and after the war was that Britain's imperial position would be inherited by Washington. And so the story continues up to modern times: however loyal Britain may have been to Clinton or to Bush in Middle Eastern military ventures, the contracts given out afterwards by grateful Gulf allies did not often come to the United Kingdom.

None of this should be a source of complaint; nations look after their own interests. It has been an American interest to swap a great deal of intelligence material with us because British signals intelligence and secret intelligence capabilities produce high quality material of use to the US. We can then trade this for information vital to our security, which their greater capability can make available. There is no sentiment in the matter, even if, as between Ian Fleming's James

Bond and Felix Leitner of the CIA, there are plenty of personal friendships. Trump's slogan, 'America First' is the reassertion (in crude form) of age-old US policy. Anyone who thinks that there is, or has ever has been, an ideological commitment in the heart of the US to free trade or to the collegiate leadership of the liberal democracies, let alone to a place of special privilege for the United Kingdom, will soon learn better when it comes to negotiating bilateral deals with an American government of any party.

It would be a very good thing if the phrase 'Special Relationship' were removed from the lexicon of clichés deployed by both British politicians and journalists, and the speech writers' notes of American presidents visiting London. Perhaps a versification of it could be set to music and sung ironically at the Last Night of the Proms, like 'Rule Britannia'. Otherwise, it should be forgotten.

Thus this Circle, real enough when a matter of genuine shared interest (such as the resistance to Soviet expansion) unites us, is a misleading image as a basis of policy where interests may conflict.

Then there was the third circle: Europe.

3　The Third Circle

As a politically conscious youngster in 1962 and 1963, I tried to engage with the subject of Europe at the time of Mr Macmillan's first attempt to take the United Kingdom into Europe. I noted that the moderate social democrat Wykehamist leader of the Labour party, Hugh Gaitskell, denounced the attempt as the ending of a thousand years of British history in his Labour party Conference speech of 1962. I noted that Sir John Winnifrith, the Permanent Secretary in the Ministry of Agriculture, vehemently opposed our abandoning the robust British system of agricultural support. Our system of 'deficiency payments' was based on taxpayers subsidising farmers in certain circumstances when world prices were too low to sustain their businesses, while letting consumers benefit from those low world prices by means of tariff-free imports. This was in terms of taxation progressive – better off tax payers subsidised farmers, the poor benefited from low world prices. The European system was the opposite; straightforwardly protectionist. Farmers were protected by keeping food prices high for all, including the poorest, by means of external tariffs. However the fundamental issue was, I thought, more important even than food prices. I still have my copy of the Treaty of Rome, 'prepared by the Foreign Office for the convenience of Parliament and the public' and published by Her Majesty's Stationery Office because of course there was no official Brussels translation into English before our and Ireland's entry.

On the first page it announces in capitals that 'HIS MAJESTY THE KING OF THE BELGIANS' and other potentates including 'HER ROYAL HIGHNESS THE GRAND DUCHESS OF LUXEMBOURG', but also the Presidents of France and West Germany, 'ARE DETERMINED TO ESTABLISH THE FOUNDA- TIONS OF AN EVER CLOSER UNION AMONG THE EUROPEAN PEOPLES...' So with the simplic- ity of youth I assumed it meant what it said, that this was a political enterprise, starting, admittedly, with the construction of economic and industrial cooperation but quite open about its ultimate objective: a union of the European peoples. This seemed a rather mag- nificent enterprise to me. I was, after all, a schoolboy classicist, who regarded the Roman Empire as a good thing and was on the side of the Emperor Claudius and his army commander Aulus Plautius when they added Britannia to the civilised world, sending the future emperor Vespasian and the Second Augustan Legion to the Mendips where I lived, and live to secure the supply of lead to be found there.

Imagine, I dreamed, a new European nation with London, Paris, Rome, Berlin and one day surely Prague and Madrid and Athens and Budapest and Warsaw as its provincial cities! An immense bastion of freedom with its culture rooted far back in my beloved ancient Greece and Rome. This was surely an ideal to work for! But steady on, I was told on all sides, this was not at all what the enterprise was about. It was purely an economic arrangement. It was called the European Economic Community, or the Common Market.

'But it says on the top ever-closer union...'

'Pay no attention, you idiot! That is just the way these European chappies talk. It is all about trade! Do you imagine the French are going to give up their sovereignty?'

That is what all the wise heads said, and went on saying. My new hero, Edward Heath, who was in charge of Mr Macmillan's application to join the EEC which was vetoed by French President de Gaulle in 1963, my later bosses and friends Margaret Thatcher, Enoch Powell,

William Rees-Mogg, Chris Patten, Michael Heseltine, Nicholas Ridley, Ken Clarke and the rest – whatever their later positions and disagreements – all told me not to worry. European federalism was for the birds. And look who is on the other side of the argument. Antediluvian nostalgic imperialists in the Monday Club; Tony Benn on the left, who, said Chris Patten in his maiden speech, always made one think of men in white coats, and the Soviet Union who claimed the whole thing was an imperialist plot.

I was judged very unsound by all wise heads for refusing a position in the Remain campaign for the referendum of 1975 and driving off with three friends to Shiraz in Iran, thereby abstaining in the vote. I could not campaign, or vote against Powell (who had by now abandoned his earlier Europeanism) and Tony Benn when they correctly argued that the Europe we were joining was a political enterprise. But I could not vote against all my friends and my former boss Edward Heath, whose political secretary I had been. It was not that I was really *against* the idea of a politically united Europe; I was just against joining it on the basis that it was something it seemed obvious to me it was not. It was never just about markets and trade. So I abstained. Not a heroic position. In retrospect, I think that my wise friends were wrong, and that they and their successors remain wrong.

First, were those socialists who argued that there was fundamental limitation of sovereignty entailed by signing the treaty of Rome, wrong? They feared that socialism in one country was effectively impossible within the structures established by Monnet and Schuman. Indeed so: those structures were explicitly designed for the purpose of embedding liberal democracy alongside free market economics in a post war Europe where both were threatened by powerful communist parties in France and Italy.

It took Enoch Powell, as he later admitted, (Robert Shepherd, *Enoch Powell, A Biography*, 1996 p. 248) some time to understand that the EEC was not just about markets, but his analysis was in the end the same as Tony Benn's and Michael Foot's: once joined, the British parliament's freedom to do whatever it chose would have gone. A good thing you may say, if, like the late Lord Hailsham you feared that parliament's untrammelled powers risked 'elective dictatorship', (*The Times,* 12 October 1968) or, like most of us, you are in favour of embedding liberal democracy and free market economics in your constitution. Though that is not quite the point. It would be Europe protecting those things for good or for ill, not the British parliament, as a result of its own sovereign choices.

There was also the 'French' argument. As Julian Jackson's magnificent biography *A Certain Idea of France* shows, de Gaulle did indeed contemplate, when he came back to power in 1958 two years after the signing of the Treaty of Rome, reversing France's commitment to the structures Jean Monnet and Robert Schuman had created, which were (and are) explicitly supra-national and designed to make a reality of the ever-closer union. In fact, he merely ensured that there should be more requirement for unanimity in European voting, a brake on integration which his successors released.

France had drawn different conclusions from Suez than the British. For the British, the conclusion was that we should not diverge too far from American leadership. For France, the lesson was that she should help to create, and should lead, a European bloc which would ultimately offer an *alternative* to American leadership. That was worth some loss of sovereignty, even in the eyes of arch-nationalist de Gaulle. France was never in doubt that the European project was a political, not just an economic undertaking, to be led of course by France, as Germany was divided and psychologically cowed. De Gaulle, when he vetoed Mr Macmillan's application on behalf of the United Kingdom, saw with his customary clarity that the British had not, in their hearts, accepted the ultimate goals of the community and regarded themselves (sometimes with American encouragement) as a sort of Trojan Horse for Atlanticism. De Gaulle was right. He understood what the narrative of the Three Circles actually meant.

There is a famous episode of *Yes, Minister*, wherein Sir Humphrey, the Permanent Secretary, explains to poor Jim Hacker, his minister, that we had joined the EEC in order to make sure it did not work – and this was not so far from the truth.

The proposal is (Jonathan Lynn and Antony Jay, *Yes Minister, The Diaries of a Cabinet Minister, Vo.l 1*, 1981) that Britain should adopt Europe-wide identity cards. Mr Hacker, the minister, is puzzled 'that such a proposal...could even be seriously under consideration by the Foreign and Commonwealth office. We can both see clearly that it is wonderful ammunition for the anti-Europeans. I asked Humphrey if the Foreign Office doesn't realise how damaging this would be to the European ideal? "I'm sure they do, Minister," he said. "That's why they support it." This was even more puzzling, since I'd always been under the impression that the FO is pro-Europe. "Is it or isn't it?" I asked Humphry. "Yes and no," he replied of course, "if you'll pardon the expression. The Foreign Office is pro-Europe because it is really anti-Europe. In fact, the Civil

Service was united in its desire to make sure the Common Market didn't work. That's why we went into it... Now that we're in we are able to make a complete pig's breakfast out of it."'

Of course, my Conservative friends were not so cynical (Sir Humphrey objected to the accusation of cynicism, 'We call it diplomacy') or not all of them, at least. However it is my contention that the British successors to the early enthusiasts, particularly the Conservative enthusiasts, did go on deluding themselves. As the European Economic Community progressed, as it had always said it would, towards ever-closer political union, via the obvious next step of the establishment of a single currency, they did not (with the exception of Powell) recognise that they had been wrong. Many claimed to have been betrayed. 'We joined a Common Market, a trading group, and it turned into a political union! No one told us this would happen!' *Really?* 'THE KING OF THE BELGIANS...'

Some pro-Europeans of course, were more subtle. They believed that the sceptical British people would come along eventually, in spite of the thousand years of history. The experience of economic, social and trading integration would generate the inevitable growth of a European political consciousness. This would quite naturally evolve into acceptance of, and then allegiance to, the supra-national institutions which underpinned such integration. To some degree they have surely been proved right; this quasi-Marxist concept of the growth of 'European consciousness' has become quite widespread, particularly amongst younger people who have lived all their lives within first the EEC and then the EU. There was and is nothing dishonourable about this cautious policy – it was a policy of leadership. There are plenty of examples of our leaders rightly introducing policies the electorate opposes, which, once introduced, that same electorate accepts: the abolition of the death penalty, for example. And after all, many of us admired how over time our own union of separate kingdoms and principalities had generated a common allegiance to Britishness. Why should the same not happen in Europe?

If our leaders had been less deterministic – less quasi-Marxist, if you like – and more explicit that the objective (slowly coming, still far ahead in time) was the voluntary creation of a new political unity, ultimately a new nation, there would surely have been a better chance of its achievement. How could the British people ever decide to commit themselves to such an objective when at every election and at the two referendums of 1975 and 2016, the narrative put before them *even by the pro Europeans* was the exact opposite? That such talk of eventual federation was nonsense, that there was no such hoped-for ultimate aim: that the trading bloc, now a monetary and increasingly legal bloc, was forever just an economic arrangement to make us richer?

Surely if the political dream had been acknowledged, defended and justified, there might have been some hope of its winning acceptance? If this was not done because our leaders understood their electorate very well, and feared that such a dream would never win allegiance at least in England, were they not guilty of helping us to sleep walk toward the United Kingdom's European crash which was crystallised, but not created, by the referendum of 2016?

In the end, surely, it was a dangerous game to say to the electorate on such a foundational issue, touching the very identity of our nation, that 'one day you will agree with us even if you do not now' and to deny that we were launched on a path of absolutely fundamental and irreversible constitutional and political change? At the very least, if you are following such a policy of stealthy subliminal persuasion, you do not risk putting it to the test of a referendum which lacked even the safety net of a 'constitutional', sixty-forty required majority, until you are certain sure you will win.

4   Is it Really About Europe at All?

My thesis is that the crisis we are in is fundamentally about Europe and our attitude to it. That the lack of candour in our leaders led to a slow-growing but inevitable dissolution of the national narrative describing our identity, which occurred when a crucial part of that narrative turned out to be false.

Let us for a moment consider some completely different explanations than that which I am offering for the Brexit constitutional and institutional crash. Some say the Brexit vote was not about Brexit at all and that it is like the Trump vote in America. It is because of quite other grievances, and the 2016 referendum was just an opportunity to kick the establishment, or the political class, or London. It is just another example of the new populism at work.

Of course, many other grievances and grumbles not directly related to Europe were, I am sure, involved in how people voted in the referendum of 2016 when it came. As Kevin O'Rourke argues in his excellent *A Short History of Brexit*, there were some short-term political choices that could have been different and might have helped lead to a different outcome. George Osborne as Chancellor of the Exchequer, it can be argued, pursued a policy of public sector austerity tighter than that followed in, say, Germany. This hit poorer people's living standards and access to services at a time when Remainers might have thought it wise to moderate pain before a referendum which could indeed be used as a general shout of protest. The Remain campaign then chose to emphasise the economic dangers of leaving, at a time when home-grown economic pain made the Leavers' largely bogus promises of a financial windfall from leaving more attractive to those people struggling with austerity.

Or, there are deep explanations for the vote that are nothing to do with Europe, provided by some of our most distinguished public intellectuals. As Hegel said, 'The owl of Minerva flies at dusk.' David Goodhart in his fascinating *The Road to Somewhere* proposed a new tribal divide between 'Somewheres' and 'Anywheres' who have lost or gained from globalisation, and overlaid this on the map of leave and remain votes (where it does not quite fit). David Runciman in *How Democracy Ends* proposes with gloomy lucidity that all manner of modern trends mean not only that all our institutions are dying, but that, 'mature, western democracy' is over the hill, so we should not be surprised if all about us is political chaos. Nonetheless, he cheers us up by proposing that 'the declining years of anyone's life are sometimes the most fulfilling,' so the last years of our polity may be quite enjoyable.

I do not think such reductionism is helpful, nor that it is right to patronise the electorate to the extent involved, in saying that they voted as they did in 2016 because of deep sociological issues of which they were not conscious, or because they used the vote simply to protest about this or that. I prefer the analysis of perhaps the most distinguished of all our current public intellectuals, John Gray. 'Screening out the continuing disintegration of the post-Cold War order is the response of liberal elites everywhere,' he writes (*New Statesman*, 13 March 2019).

Yes, many people were angry that for a number of years most people's net incomes had been going up very little or not at all, particularly in areas where globalisation of trade had hastened the decline of older industries. Yes, the other marked effect of globalisation, that inequalities between those able to profit from it and those not able to do so, widened. Yes, some doubtless felt left behind or in the old jargon alienated from a 'political class' which did not seem to be interested in such anxieties. Certainly, social media allows unhappy groups to band together and reinforce each other's unhappiness. Yes, some were doubtless taken in by some straightforward lies told by the Leave campaign.

And yes, there was ever-present accident and luck. There is nothing inevitable about the movement of history. Boris Johnson might have campaigned on the other side (always unlikely: he rightly saw his chance of succeeding his old enemy Cameron to be better if he rode the rising wave of Leave sentiment within the Conservative party, even if, as I suspect he believed, Cameron were to win his referendum). Cameron might have called the referendum later; Labour might have been led by a genuine and persuasive Remainer, rather than the antique Marxists Ed Miliband (another of The Guilty Men, perhaps) had helped into the leadership of his party. And so on. However, my instinct is that it was not really any of that – it was because what I have called our 'national narrative' was disintegrating around us and the Europe which had been sold to us was a central part of that narrative which now no longer worked.

After all, there had been lies at previous elections, periods of austerity after periods of fast growth before, complaints about the remoteness of leaders from the people since Pericles and Cleon scrapped in fifth century BC Athens.

I voted remain, because I felt in my children the growth of that very European identity which no mainstream politicians had felt called upon to champion. But my pen hovered for a moment over the other box as a way of marking my protest that, in my view, no one had told the truth about what it meant to commit ourselves to Europe. We had not been told from the moment we had first applied, and we as former imperialists should understand better than anyone that people will vote to be poorer if it means they are free, so the whole Remain campaign had fought on the wrong ground. If I hesitated, how much more strongly must those have been pulled towards Leave who had benefitted much less from globalisation than I had, working as I had done since 1997 in the City of London?

At the back of my mind also was a more pragmatic, perhaps Machiavellian, reason for voting to remain. Thanks to the negotiating skills of John Major and the obduracy of Gordon Brown, Britain had not joined the Euro and would not for the foreseeable future. Meanwhile, Britain's demography was markedly different from that of other big European countries. This was because of immigration, both from outside the EU and, after 2005 and the admission of many eastern European countries, from within the Union. Immigrants naturally tend to be younger and not only increase populations themselves but add children once they have settled. On plausible projections, another twenty years might make the United Kingdom the biggest economy in Europe, not because of superior productivity but because of the size of our population. So even if we were still really playing Sir Humphrey's devious nationalist game of disruption, why not wait?

Why not wait to see whether we might become more comfortable with our growing, but semi-detached power within Europe? Why not leave it to Brussels to try to force changes in that semi-detached status if they began to resent it more and more, as they were showing signs of doing, while we could fight the obstructionist battles de Gaulle had predicted we would fight all those years ago, with all the ammunition available to us that full membership provided? But disgruntled democracies are difficult creatures to which to preach patience and the virtues of a hidden long-term strategy. Nor was Prime Minister Cameron, in many ways an excellent, liberally-minded Conservative leader for the times, a man much given to long-term planning. A referendum to settle it for Remain seemed the easier way – after all, his government had already won two referendums for the status quo, on Scotland and the voting system. Why not gamble on a third victory?

Cameron will always be condemned by Remainers and by constitutionalists, for the gamble of this second European referendum. However, we should have a little more sympathy for a leader who gambles: 635,000 votes out of 33,600,000 the other way and as I write, he would very likely still be Prime Minister and lauded throughout Europe as the brave but democratic leader who faced down Nigel Farage and sent Boris Johnson back to journalism. As for gambling: did not Churchill gamble wildly in 1940? Who could have been so mad as to assume Hitler would attack Russia before defeating us? Or that Germany would be stupid enough to let its loyalty to its ally Japan cause it to declare war on the United States after Pearl Harbour? But Churchill's gamble worked and his place among the greatest of all leaders is assured.

So we voted to leave, by a lesser margin than some might have expected if you accept my argument that our commitment to the real and open European project had never been truly sought or given, so perhaps the Remain campaign was not as badly fought as all that. That being said, the vote meant that the last of our Three Circles was broken. There was no national narrative, and collateral damage in all directions.

5   Collateral Damage

OF COURSE, THE REFERENDUM itself was a gamble not just in relation to the outcome, but in relation to the interaction of its result with our constitutional parliamentary democracy. In 1975, no such acute conflict emerged, though it could have done, because the decisive vote to Remain – universal throughout the kingdom with the exception of the Western Isles of Scotland – reflected the opinion of the majority in the House of Commons. It was in scale decisive enough for mild Leavers honourably and genuinely to accept its verdict, even if the more determined among them continued (rightly from their point of view, and perhaps ours) to prophesy doom. This time, the much narrower result combined with the fact that all four main parties had – somewhat perfunctorily in the case of Labour – campaigned to Remain (as that was the preference of the majority of their MPs) has led to a severe crisis of confidence. Not only is this crisis in the most important institution of all, Parliament, but in almost all our other institutions. The ensuing chaos threatens not only them, but also the cautious and long-standing political culture which has underpinned them.

First, let us consider parliament. Parliamentary democracy is meant to work like a jury. From time immemorial – long before political democracy – we have resisted the idea that anyone accused of a crime should be judged by the mob. Twelve citizens should look into the case carefully, hear both sides, and deliver a considered verdict. So too is the process with parliament and parliamentary parties. An MP, as the Irishman Edmund Burke put it, owes to his constituents 'not his industry only, but his judgement; and he betrays, instead of serving you, if he sacrifices it to your opinion.' MPs should be representatives, not delegates. It is true that the electors of Bristol to whom he delivered this doctrine did not much care for it, and Burke had to retire to a pocket borough of Lord Rockingham's, but prophets are often without honour close to home, particularly in Bristol.

A proposition put to parliament should be considered carefully, even a proposition endorsed by the monarch, or in today's terms, by the sovereign people. The people might conceivably vote that the earth is flat – a large internet community believes that it is – but that does not make it so, and parliament should point this out. If the people continue in their flat earth belief, well then, they must elect a new parliament they hope will not have read Copernicus or Kepler.

We have been somewhat in that position since the referendum. We have voted for Brexit, having been told that it was a pretty straightforward matter. A deal to facilitate leaving, said Leavers, would be easily forthcoming because it was in everyone's best interest. This did not turn out to be so. Perhaps the Leavers had forgotten that the institutions of the EU had a very considerable interest in not making it easy for member states to leave – no political entity likes to undermine the principles on which it is founded. After all, remember 'His Majesty the King of the Belgians...' and so on. And a number of other countries did not share France's deep scepticism about British commitment: they saw Britain as a vital component of a liberal Europe, which they desperately hoped would remain if enough obstacles were put in our way. After all, surely the British were above all pragmatists?

Surely the British had not forgotten all about the Northern Irish border, the brilliant fuzziness of the Good Friday agreement which allowed the various communities in the province and across the border which had fought so viciously for decades, if not centuries, to live within a structure where they could choose the identity they preferred within a cross-border European framework? How could maintaining that outcome be reconciled with the obvious need for the EU to protect its single market if a tariff border with all its concomitant police and customs posts was once more in place between the Republic and Northern Ireland?

Theresa May's government, banging its head against these difficulties, negotiated a deal with Europe for the first stage of our exit which did not find favour in parliament because some thought it a bad deal for keeping us too close to Europe, whilst some did not want to leave at all, and others thought that the duty of an opposition was to oppose, come what may. So parliament had voted to leave out of respect for the referendum result, but failed to agree on how this should be done, or indeed what leaving actually meant.

It is therefore unsurprising that this unique failure of parliament has bred deep frustration and damaged the reputation of the institution and its members. Many in parliament take the referendum vote as equivalent to a vote that the earth is flat and think it perfectly in order to try to have it reversed; others accept the verdict, but cannot agree how best to bring it into practical effect. Parliament appears to have failed.

Meanwhile in another direction, abandonment of

the 'jury' model in our representative democracy has arguably made matters even worse. Previously MPs were allowed, with some advice from outside interests, to be the best judges of each other's merits. Now, limited party memberships are sovereign, or nearly so, and the further from real knowledge of the candidates for party leadership, the clearer are the opinions of those who have the decisive votes. At the moment when the institution of parliament is in stasis and unable to decide what to do, the leaders of the two biggest traditional parties would neither of them, in my judgement, have been elected in a secret ballot of those colleagues who know them best, if those colleagues had constituted the only electorate, and had not had to look for their survival in constituency selection meetings to the favour of members who knew the candidates much less well than did the MPs. Perhaps this does not matter.

Perhaps Corbyn and Johnson will surprise us all with their wisdom and their capacity to lead. This curious, semi-populist symmetry in the way our present main party leaders have been chosen is not, of course, anything to do with Brexit, but the similarity of the strain put on internal party procedures by a mixture of direct and indirect democracy is rather like the much greater strain put on parliamentary democracy in the same way by the use of referendums.

It seems clear that the collapse of acceptance of the Third Circle, Europe, in the manner of its happening, has delivered a dreadful blow to our once secure allegiance to parliament. Who can have allegiance to an institution that does nothing?

Lesser, but still significant collateral damage has been done to other institutions we trusted and about whose effectiveness we boasted. Since entry to the European Union it is true that on the whole departments of state staffed by civil servants, whatever the opinions of individual officials, have taken the view that foreign and constitutional policy cannot be changed every five years (as they would not then be foreign or constitutional policy). They also took the view that the UK had committed itself after a decisive referendum and with the support of all subsequent governments, to Europe and its institutions. Thus, officials could take it that continuing membership of Europe was a given. I know for a fact that there remained, perhaps particularly in the Treasury, some whose personal views like those of Sir John Winnifrith long ago, were not instinctively pro-European, vitally in relation to membership of the currency union. There were plenty who were as irritated by EU bureaucracies as anyone else and a good many more who took Sir Humphrey's view that our job was to slow down or dilute European enthusiasm for federalism, so that the objective became a can kicked down a very long and winding road. Overall, however, Britain's policy was settled: we would remain members of the EU.

To ask the public service to reverse its view, literally overnight, was a very big ask, particularly if a good many of those doing the asking appeared not to have thought much about the costs and difficulties. The civil service has done its best to adjust to the new reality, but it would be natural if warnings of the dire consequences of leaving were not more passionately believed than the new doctrines of the Leavers that all would be well in the new world. That is indeed so in all times of change. Machiavelli again, 'The innovator has for enemies all those who have done well under the old conditions, and lukewarm defenders in those who may do well under the new.' So the civil service, while loyally doing its job, has grumbled, and for this natural grumbling been very bitterly attacked by the Leavers, causing another great British institution to be damaged.

The same thing has happened to the Bank of England, normally far above the political fray. When its admirable governor, Mark Carney published, as was his duty, various theoretical scenarios (including very unpleasant scenarios) in order to ensure that the financial system was prepared for every contingency, he was traduced as if he was claiming that those scenarios were the outcome he predicted and for allegedly fighting on the Remain side of the argument. And so another institution took on water, damaged by those who should have known better.

And the Law? Perhaps our greatest glory and the most convincing of all arguments for scepticism about Europe, in that many sensible people resent the encroachment of European styles of law making on our genuinely ancient and powerful tradition of common law – did the law escape undamaged in the melee? Certainly not. The Leavers, briefing their favourite newspaper of the time, the *Daily Mail*, cast the judges of the Supreme Court 'as enemies of the people' no less, for a very common-sense judgement about the degree to which the executive, the government, may make fundamental policy without parliament (the very same sort of argument incidentally that the Leavers deployed themselves in relation to the infringement of parliamentary prerogatives by European law). The result is that even the independence of the judiciary has come under threat.

One institution beloved above all others at present may even be involved in the chaos. Some say that the interaction of the badly-conceived 2011 Fixed-term Parliaments Act with the conflicts in Parliament over whether or not a Prime Minister has a right to dissolve that Parliament at the time he or she wants if he or she are defeated, it might put the Queen and her advisers also in the political firing line. If a Conservative Prime Minister were to achieve that, their consignment to the dustbin of history would indeed be well merited. Let us hope that this risk is remote.

All this collateral damage can in time be repaired. We have seen worse constitutional and institutional chaos in our history. This is not worse than King James II fleeing the country in 1688, throwing the Great Seal in the Thames as he went in a futile attempt to stop executive government. This is not 1745, with a French backed army advancing from Scotland to Derby. *Habeas corpus* has not been suspended for fear of sedition or revolution as in 1794 or 1817. As Sir Simon Jenkins has pointed out in his column in the Guardian newspaper, we may count it a success so far at least that there has been very little political violence directly attributable to our Brexit arguments, though arguably there has been some and could be more.

Nonetheless, the generalised collateral damage is real, and adds to our feelings that this crisis is deeper and more dangerous than anything in our recent history. Some, of course, delight in the disruption. The extreme left, for example, who hate settled institutions for obvious reasons; the childish 'disruptors' who believe that throwing things in the air is good fun, and those who despise settled institutions for the sort of reasons the fascists and communists despised them in the thirties – as roadblocks in their paths to power. But those who understand how difficult is the construction of the settled institutions of a liberal democracy, and know with de Jouvenel that if institutions do not to some degree have halos around them then they will need more policemen (de Jouvenel, *Sovereignty*, 1957) – such people take a different view. Damaged institutions, their halos lost, will certainly need more policemen before trust and allegiance is rebuilt.

One further element of our stability over many years has also suffered. That stability has, to the annoyance of many reformers, been based on the electorate's willingness to push politicians into two broad alliances of leftist and rightist colour before elections. The first-past-the-post system compels this: a broad alliance forged before an election can form a stable government, the winner having taken all. The British have seemed to prefer this to coalitions put together afterwards, as they often have to be in countries which use proportional voting systems. If first-past-the-post works, it works well. It means that you know above all what to do to turn the rapscallions out – you vote for the other lot. In other countries you may change your party vote only to find that your new party has made a post- election deal with the very rapscallions you wanted to eject in the first place.

For many years in the twentieth century a broad alliance of a significant minority of the working class with a majority of the middle class made up the Conservative party; the mirror image formed Labour. Somewhat more conservative social policy and a reputation for economic competence fought it out with somewhat more progressive social policy and riskier public spending habits. The European divide, however, has smashed those structures: Labour working-class Leavers are allied with rural Conservatives and the elderly, big business and most of the City of London with Scottish nationalists and left-leaning Hampstead-intellectual Remainers and the cosmopolitan conurbation including most of its younger and more educated citizens. The academic analysis is fluid and not yet complete, but it is easy to show that the Leave/Remain divide bears no relation to old party structures. Liberal Democrats now pitch to represent all Remainers, regardless of whether they hold otherwise liberal views: the Brexit party and the Conservatives and part of the Labour party fight for the votes of Leavers.

These times are frightening for the supporters of all the old parties, but perhaps most for Labour: there was always something contingent about the alliance between the left-of-centre middle class with the working class, and it is just possible that the Leave/Remain divide, at least while it lasts, propels that left-of-centre middle class back to where it came from, the Liberal party, leaving the Conservatives, at least temporarily, with the votes of more of those who self-identify as 'working class' to add to the quarter or third of such people whom the Tories always managed to attract.

Are we about to see the Strange Rebirth of Liberal England, in reversal of the title of George Dangerfield's famous book of 1935? Liberal Democrats might claim to be the only nation-wide Remain party – and collect unionists votes into the bargain by arguing that Remain is less dangerous to the union than Leave.

Meanwhile, a Labour party fighting to prevent this by a whole-hearted shift to Remain might find itself contributing to the growth of a formidable new Brexit-based conservative alliance – if the Conservatives could find convincing leaders to demonstrate their commitment to those 'left behind' Labour Leave voters. But there is a similar danger for the Tories. If they showed their colours on issues such as immigration and redistribution to the lower-paid in order to attract former Labour Leavers, would they not also contribute voters from their middle class south to this new Liberal party?

Scotland, fairly solidly Remain, allies its nationalism to Europe; nationalists in England to Brexit. Hardline unionists in Northern Ireland fight for Brexit, although the province voted Remain and might, given the chance, prefer to join the now secular and liberal Republic rather than follow England and Wales into a hard Brexit. The old first-past-the-post dualism is, for the time being, utterly broken; no one, least of all the political pundits, can predict the outcome of a general election called against such a background. Wondering foreigners see chaos in the home of what was arguably the western world's most stable and predictable democracy, and they, like the rest of us, cannot see how it ends.

6   Systemic Damage

CITIZENS NOTICE IF THOSE who are ruling them have no plan and no sense of direction. This is true of any community: a family, a firm, a school, a profession, a neighbourhood. Shared purpose and confidence that decision-takers have some continuing strategy allows one to leave them to it so that the rest of us can get on with our lives.

The sense that since 1945, with many a stop and start, the direction of our national affairs externally has been competent and broadly sensible, built trust. For most of this time this trust has extended (with many a failing and plenty of argument) to a broad belief that our leaders and our institutions would, all in all, deliver policies which helped us, or at least not hinder us much, from living more prosperous lives supported by improving public services. Machiavelli recommended in *The Prince* that a government having serious trouble at home should consider adventurism abroad. One might turn his advice around and say that if things are going on reasonably at home, a settled and stable policy abroad will be seen as an extension of the competence at home.

To put it another way, though our highly developed sense of political satire would seldom let it be recognised, Britain has on the whole been rather well governed since the Second World War, at home and abroad. Modern scholarship, for example Robert Tombs's magisterial *The English and their History* shows that our fashion for believing in our own decline has been much overdone.

Such objective comparative measures that exist of national well being show us as being rather happy, compared to most nations. We also normally score rather highly in measures which claim to say which nations are admired by others abroad, but not too much weight should be placed on such league tables. Though the steady demand from people from other parts of the world to come to settle here, to be educated here, to speak our language and buy our cultural products tells the same story. Never for a moment would we say so out loud, but in spite of all in the last three quarters of a century we have not been too far from John Major's ideal of a nation at ease with itself. The big current anxieties, for example: the increase of perceived inequalities; worries for many about incomers taking our jobs; the immediate pain, whether necessary or not, of the austerity after 2010 and its effect on public services; how best to respond to the threat of climate change – all these would be capable of a reasonable response by institutions which had seen us through before, if there had not been a sudden and lurching fear that the institutions themselves had suffered such severe damage that they might not now deserve our allegiance.

It was this trust in our imperfect institutions (much more imperfect then, of course) which Marx did not really understand, good journalist though he was. People will put up with a very great deal if they think they live in a competently-run country where the myriad improvements they can see to be needed have, in their view, a reasonable route to improvement, through institutions they trust. However, if the institutions fail – if a big war is lost, if a central policy turns out to have been built on sand, or if allegiance has been accorded to a false king – there is likely to be trouble. In fact, inequalities in Britain have changed little in recent years, and are little different from those in, say, France or Germany. We do not have the extraordinary inequalities of China, or India or the United States. This issue can be handled.

All the evidence indicates that so long as the institutions which provide fundamental countervailing equalities are seen to be steadily improving and providing reasonable access to good services, most people will not worry a great deal about the inevitable fact that some are much richer than others, some have more luck than others and some are happier or more beautiful than others. If reasonable healthcare, education and access to law, for example, are provided for everyone, then most evidence seems to show that people accept the fact that freedom will produce very different outcomes for different people, sometimes as the result of merit and sometimes as the result of luck.

John Rawls, the great Harvard moral philosopher, proposed in his modernisation of older social contract theory, *A Theory of Justice*, a 'Rawls test' by which we may try to judge whether a society is acceptably fair. If we could not know in advance what position we might take in that society, how much inequality would we accept in it? It seems that, judged by such measures of happiness we have of different societies, the answer is 'quite a lot' if the inequality is seen as the inevitable concomitant of personal liberty. But not too much, and not too much liberty, either. Social contract theory has all sorts of logical difficulties, but as a rule of thumb, something like the Rawls test seems to be useful – but it relies, I would argue, on people trusting that there are institutions which are effective in shifting the balance back to a better equilibrium if things seem to have gone out of balance. If they lose confidence in the institutions which mediate and rebalance, things can become dangerous very quickly.

It took the citizens of my old constituency city of Bristol to chase the Bishop across the rooftops and cut up the civic plate at the defeat of the first Reform Bill in 1831 to ensure the passage of the second Reform Bill in 1832, after all. After that slow (sometimes very slow) progress on the franchise resumed. The civic plate, which had not been melted down but simply thrown into the river, was retrieved, pieced together again and replaced on the Lord Mayor's sideboard, where it remains. The Bishop is now, of course, a leader of progressive thought. That is, perhaps, not a bad metaphor for how a nation should reform itself, and rebuild.

The financial crash of 2008 itself was not enough to shatter trust in the institutions of the state. Such events had happened before, and the response from the authorities on this occasion, not least thanks to the contribution of our then Prime Minister Gordon Brown, was far more effective than for example it had been in the late 1920s and early 1930s. Within five years of the terrible slump of 2009 following the crash of 2008,

GDP per head had recovered in the UK. In those years, there was bitterness, anger and genuine tragedy in every nation, but good arguments were deployed and practical action taken in every democracy as national finances were restored, with great pain to many people – but an astonishingly low level of civil violence.

Within a decade, without the artificial stimulus of rearmament for war as in the 1930s, there was and is real hope of a return to steady improvement for most people in most advanced and many developing economies. However, a huge extra strain had to be taken by democratic institutions mediating the inevitably bitter arguments about the best way forward – in Britain, France, the US, Ireland, Greece, Scandinavia, Italy, Japan and everywhere where liberal democracy, that highest of all technologies of government, was well established.

Britain has done no worse than others in weathering this storm, and better than some, though the Conservatives were rash to attempt to combine a return to financial stability with a diminution of the role of the state. This meant that those services on which the social contract of the nation depends were under huge strain at a time when they were most needed. Such rebalancing, needed from time to time (I believe as a Conservative) should be done in the upswing periods when everyone is gaining, and not at a time of such social and economic stress. That mistake – a 'business as usual' mistake normally corrected by a change of heart by a sitting government, or its replacement by one a step or two to the left – does not explain the depth of our political crisis now.

The crisis now feels much deeper than it has felt before because for the first time, perhaps for centuries, we fear our institutions are failing us and that our national narrative no longer convinces us. Our post-Second World War settlement, in the Three Circles narrative and its concomitant membership of the European Union, has collapsed, and the collapse has severely damaged our most trusted civil institutions. These institutions have then failed in their primary task of the mediation of strongly-held opposing views.

On the one hand, there is the passion – real passion – which many feel in opposition to the loss of sovereignty implied by membership of the EU. On the other, equivalent anger is felt by those – a minority certainly, but not a trivial minority – who do believe in the slow-growing concept of European allegiance. Then there is a third group, perhaps bigger than either of the other two. I would predict this third force will now quite swiftly emerge. As the country appears to be heading for a very disruptive departure from arrangements which have grown organically at every level of life since we joined Europe four decades ago, there is an additional source of anger, and potentially bitter anger, derived from people who have up to now not been much interested in pro- or anti-European sentiments. They have trusted that the institutions would produce some sensible outcome amid the usual clamour of parliamentary dispute, media hysteria and overblown political rhetoric, and it has not happened.

Non-political people have got used to shutting out this sort of noise at every election. They are used to being told that this is the most important election since time began, that Thatcher, Blair, Major, Brown, Cameron or May, or whoever it is, are the worst leaders ever known, illustrated by Scarfe cartoons showing every politician to be an enormous evil slug, with insults ranging from the Tories as 'vermin' (Aneurin Bevan) to the absurdity of a warning that electing Labour risked a new Gestapo (Churchill) and nowadays every satirical show ramps up the shrillness of its invective in order to get airtime. The electorate has been rather good at shutting it all out and voting calmly at the end of the clamorous ritual. But now? They have shut out the noise and got on with life, and the usual, reasonably safe and boring outcome has not transpired. The institutions are failing to deliver compromise and an enormous discontinuity suddenly seems imminent.

Citizens have faced this before, above all in September 1939. But the long, slow, descent to war at that time had the appearance of inevitability. Neville Chamberlain had gone to the farthest possible lengths – and beyond – to avoid it. Under those circumstances and with a fortitude that remains extraordinary and extraordinarily honourable, the British people dug air-raid shelters, handed gasmasks to their children, and prepared again for the horrors most adults among the population remembered from between 1914 and 1918.

A precipitous falling-out of 40-year-old arrangements for trade, travel, health and culture does not feel like the end point of that dreadful slow march to an inevitable but honourable war against Hitler and Mussolini, at least to a large number of our fellow citizens. It feels like crass incompetence. A great number of our fellow citizens are threatened with the discovery that actual, immediate things they value and on which they depend are likely to be taken away from them: whether they be grand scientists in European cooperative programmes, Somerset sheep farmers who rely on exports to France, car workers whose components for assembly come from half a dozen different European sources, or those involved in a million other relationships they have taken for granted for forty years and more which may now, and suddenly, be severely disrupted.

For these people, who may not care one way or the other very much about sovereignty, or the European project, face immediate loss: and they may become very angry indeed. People do, when you take things they value away from them without a compelling reason for doing so. Very many people will see no compelling reason for the significant disruption of their lives if such comes about, and they will be angry. So, the Brexit ditch, whatever happens, is going to be a very uncomfortable obstacle to cross and when it has passed, one way or another, anger, recrimination and bitterness will be widespread and damage to our institutions serious.

I have no magic path across the battlefield to suggest. What must now be addressed in good time is the question, where next? Where do we go next to find a plausible alternative national narrative, which can provide that national standing ground on which to rebuild damaged institutions, and how can we begin to propose a better future for all those suddenly awake to the danger of the disruption of their way of life by a process they assumed our institutions would mediate?

Normally when there is a shift of direction or a

sharp discontinuity in the affairs of a nation, it is because one faction with a plan has wrested power from an incumbent faction trying to defend a different status quo. Thus, the anti-Catholic faction (with a little help from the Dutch secret service) drove James II out; the Tories ended Marlborough's involvement in European dynastic politics and turned Britain out to the blue water; Peel dismantled agricultural protection and reinforced the growth of Britain as an industrial power with cheaper food and higher living standards for the workers – and so on. One paradigm replaced another. But now? The foolish and fashionable doctrine of 'disruption' proposes that from the destruction of one paradigm another will automatically grow, more advanced than its predecessor. In the life of nations, as in other spheres, there is nothing inevitable about improvement.

Nations and peoples may go backwards for centuries if their response to new challenges is inadequate. A long period of dominance by Muslim powers in the eastern Mediterranean and south-central Asia up to the sixteenth century was followed by a long period of retreat only now perhaps beginning to end. Spain lost a world-leading position in the eighteenth century without successfully restoring its sense of identity until the

7   Can Normal Service Be Resumed?

LET US REMIND OURSELVES of what is being disrupted and consider whether the disruption may simply pass. Let us consider the First Circle, our 'Special Relationship' with the US, embedded in NATO but for the purposes of our national narrative simply described as the Special Relationship. NATO derived its legitimacy from the genuine need to resist the expansion of Stalinist Communism in Europe and elsewhere. It was not a fantasy to imagine that Stalin and his only slightly less dreadful successors meant exactly what their 1945 slogan 'onwards to the west' said. It is hard now to remember how many apologists, some of them paid for by the Soviets, attempted to undermine the necessary solidarity of the west in the face of aggression and subversion by the perpetrators of the Katyn massacre, of the Gulag, and the torture chambers of the KGB. What is easier to recall is the stalwart solidarity of the huge majority across the political and social spectrum, from social democrats to conservatives, which in the end prevailed.

However, from the moment of the dissolution of the Soviet European empire, NATO began to lose the power it derived from the simplicity of its mission. As a player in a more traditional multipolar diplomacy it may still have a role to play. Europe's relationship to its Russian neighbour will ultimately surely become a matter for Europeans to decide as Americans ask themselves what exactly their interest would be in, say, conflict with Russia over Ukrainian borders or Georgian independence.

Indeed one current member of NATO at the time of writing, Turkey, seems as close to Russia as it does to America. Then there are the immense tectonic geopolitical shifts taking place around the world. China's relationship to America and to Russia, to Europe, to India and to Japan; Europe and America's responses – all this seems far beyond the scope of an alliance founded in the bipolar world of the 1950s. The rise of Africa, whose huge population by the end of this century will match those of the other continental behemoths of India and China, will be generating issues for

Europe quite different from any which it may raise for the United States.

To attempt to interest the United States in the re-building of what has been for years a largely imaginary Special Relationship with Britain against the background of this changing world seems, to put it mildly, an ambitious project. President Trump, in his crude way, has reminded those with eyes to see and ears to hear that the United States has no sentiment in relation to its foreign policy other than its own self interest (and is no different from any other sovereign state in that). Arguably, he has done us a service in Britain by saying so.

The Commonwealth? India will be by far the most important nation of the Commonwealth should that organisation survive another quarter of a century or so – an outcome rather pleasingly foreshadowed by the Indians taking control of the Commonwealth's unique sport, cricket. Many useful second order things are still undertaken by the loose Commonwealth association of nations in culture, education, sport, and, for example, in the field of mutual aid if there is a natural disaster. No one can feel ill will towards the organisation, particularly while Queen Elizabeth II reigns. Its invention has helped Britain in the transition from Empire, and in some cases it has been useful to former colonies too. Though no-one can believe that India, Pakistan,

Canada, Australia, New Zealand, Nigeria or any other member will design their futures around a framework of former British imperial connections. All international networks which spread civilised behaviour and offer voluntary fora for cooperation must be good, the Commonwealth among them. No one can do other than applaud good people who do good things under its aegis, but it is not a player in the great game of nations and of continents, nor in the next years will it satisfy in particular our British need for a sense of identity, any more than can a hankering for the 'Special Relationship'.

And then Europe. As I have argued, Britain was sold a prospectus which was false and the opportunity was lost to tackle the immense task of building an allegiance to a new continental power with Britain as a component. Perhaps it would never have succeeded: but it was never tried, except by little clubs of enthusiasts more akin to those who used to proselytise for Esperanto than to activists who generate real movements of power. The falsity of the prospectus which was deployed led to increasing irritation, and irritation to powerful opposition. Finally, the demand that we have another say as a people, in which our allegiance to the true prospectus should be tested once and for all was granted by David Cameron; he gambled, and the referendum was both lost and won. The winning disruptors had no plan. Their persuasiveness came from the fact that they were telling one big truth about the fact that we were members of an organisation whose fundamental direction we did not share.

The damage they have done derives from the number of lies they told, deliberately or not, along the way, above all about the ease of leaving the organisation and then forging a new relationship with it and the rest of the world without significant difficulty. Their shots at a future narrative were and are thin in the extreme. The best the Leavers could do was 'global Britain' or 'Singapore-on-Thames' or a miraculous maintenance of all the convenient parts of the status quo without the inconvenient parts.

Remainers were little better: no powerful voice argued straightforwardly that we should go fully for it. Join the European enterprise because our old alliances were dying and a new world of immense continental blocs is being born – all of whom will listen only to voices of power. No one said that nations of our size often cannot defend their citizens from the coming threats. Instead, Remainers gave us the old story: ever-closer union is only words (and Cameron has got us exempted from them anyway). It is not really political but economic and we will be poorer if we leave. Because their argument was ultimately false (except, probably, in its derided 'Project Fear' which told us that we would at least for a time be poorer), they lost.

Well, the disruptors won. The first two circles died of inanition and the third collapsed because it would not fight on the only ground on which it could win: that of the stark truth. Of course, it might not have won on that either. That is why the political chaos of the next months will be so bitter. Our national narrative has collapsed, severely damaging trust in our institutions, and it cannot be revived. There is no normal service to which we can return.

Now we have no story to tell ourselves, no 'lie to bind' as Kwame Anthony Appiah calls the multiple narratives around which we define our identity in *The Lies that Bind*. We will need one, if we are to stay a people bound into a nation, and to rebuild our institutions. Possibilities of such stories exist, but who will tell them to us in ways that we might believe? And what do we have to pass through before such a story can be crafted?

8   Stories, Bad and Magical

THERE ARE BAD STORIES which can take hold of a nation as well as good, and they can be horribly dangerous. After 1919, partly owing to the foolish but liberal beneficence of Woodrow Wilson in allowing an honourable armistice rather than fighting on for a more dramatic surrender, the myth grew in Germany that their army had never been defeated. This was completely false. The extent and completeness of Allied victories on and after what Ludendorff correctly called 'the black day of the German Army' (8 August 1918) has been forgotten in a Britain which prefers to commemorate the horrors of the Somme. With American strength hardly committed and the German population half starved, a more ruthless Alliance could have demilitarised Germany then as happened in 1945. Instead, a military 'armistice' followed by punitive reparations helped to create a dreadful narrative in Germany that a stab in the back had betrayed an undefeated military and that ruthless allies had taken advantage of this for their own profit. The seeds were sown for 1939, but before seeking revenge this time the 'undefeated' militarist Germany would first eliminate those it claimed as being responsible for the stab in the back of 1918. So, out of pre-existing antisemitism, the Holocaust was born and the murder of communists and social democrats, too.

There is one narrative today in Britain that could be almost equally dangerous. If a myth becomes established that a great popular victory to leave Europe, won in the teeth of the establishment, has been betrayed by a 'deep state' or by other trickery, the alienation of some sizeable minority at least of our people from the institutions judged to have been responsible for such a betrayal could run very deep.

I am not saying, of course, that what would happen would be a rerun of what happened in Germany between the wars, but we could live in a deeply divided country for many years, with consequences that would be corrosive of civil society. Something like this followed from the divisions in France derived from the Vichy-Gaullist split, and they have still to fully play out in that magnificent country. Does this mean that the hard-line Remainers must have their way, come what may? No, but it does mean that any direction which does not look compatible with the result of the 2016 referendum, or a development from it, must be treated with extreme caution.

There could certainly be no reversal of that decision without another referendum, and the dangers that way are very great, since no one can guarantee what its outcome would be. The prospect of an infinite regress of referendums, with ever more damage to our institutions and to civil society, would be real. Who would win the second one? If Leavers again, an even more bitter campaign might have triggered an unstoppable drive towards a second referendum in Scotland. Perhaps even in Northern Ireland a powerful drive towards unification with the Republic might emerge. If the original verdict was reversed and Remainers won, perhaps on a lower poll, the betrayal myth would have been born. Thus, a second referendum is extremely high risk. There is no magic way of going back to square one: of waking up as if after a bad dream to find things back as they were before 2016. On the contrary, there is the very considerable danger of making present divisions even worse.

I am writing this against the background of fast moving events: Boris Johnson arriving at Downing St, the construction of a hard-line Leaver government, and a final attempt by the Conservative party to deliver Brexit. With less than one hundred days to achieve it, the new Prime Minister and his principal colleagues have committed themselves to ensuring Brexit by 31 October 2019. They know that there is no Parliamentary majority for a hard, no-deal Brexit. They know that they will find it impossible with this parliament, and before 31 October, to pass much of the legislation needed to mitigate the effects of no deal, for example on farmers. Their twin-track approach might possibly be to try some radically new advance to Europe designed by Michael Gove and Dominic Cummings, both of whom are genuinely clever lateral thinkers. This could perhaps progress along the lines of a proposal to leave on 31 October while the whole United Kingdom remains within a free-trade area for, say, two years, while a different future relationship is agreed. This or some more sophisticated alternative, would of course face immense difficulties of delivery: those Leavers whose intellectual capacities Mr Cummings is on record as not rating very highly would block it one way, and the ponderous institutions of the EU in another. Such a failure would be likely to make the atmosphere in No. 10 very rancorous, as Matthew Parris has predicted, and some other strategy would have to emerge.

Failing the appearance of such a magical policy, the government will presumably stick to the other track which it sometimes describes merely as a policy designed to awaken concessions from Europe: 'no deal' mitigated by as many bilateral 'side deals' as possible. Concessions of substance from Europe seem unlikely, though not quite impossible. If no deal is the outcome, it would be very unlikely to get through the present parliament which would then attempt either to bring the government down or to change the law compelling us to leave on 31 October. Perhaps it might even attempt to withdraw the Article 50 application to leave altogether. If the Johnson Government faced defeat on either a no-confidence motion, or a bill to change the present default leaving date, it would presumably take the initiative and call an election.

Meanwhile an almost equal anger, slower to grow but no less profound, will emerge from those who have woken up to the fact that a no-deal Brexit means real, practical, financial and other loss. This is perhaps the sleeping giant of British opinion as I write: constituted of those very many people for whom, in spite of the noise, Brexit has remained secondary in their lives because they assumed that our leaders and our famed institutions would deliver some tolerable compromise which would not affect them too much. If they begin to doubt that such an outcome is to be delivered, their anger could be as great as those of the other groups, the more politicised Remainers, and the Leavers.

It seems to me that whatever happens – apart from the magical outcome to which I will return – we have a further very deep and sulphurous ditch to cross before anyone will have the chance to attend to generating a plausible new narrative for Britain. It would be a hard task to attempt to craft a story that might achieve widespread currency and begin a slow process of inching back towards a country living reasonably at ease with itself, with institutions trusted to ameliorate the many areas of life (as in any country) which need it. Let us depress ourselves a little by peering into the sulphurous ditch we must cross.

We imagine later this year, a situation not solved by magic, but a Johnson government delivering nothing in the way of a new deal, and bound by its commitment to leave on 31 October. The pound is by now probably at parity with the dollar and the economy more or less stopped. Mr Johnson manages to call an election, which like Mr Heath in February 1974, he will attempt to fight on one issue. This time, it is not, 'Who rules: Parliament or the trades unions?', but 'Who rules, your will as expressed in the referendum, or a Parliament of betrayers?'

There is one difficult complication before this election could be called. If the Prime Minister wanted to ask for an election because the government faced defeat on a bill to extend the 31 October date, whether by withdrawing Article 50 or in some other way, then under Mr Cameron's ill-thought-out Fixed-term Parliaments Act, there is, I suppose, a theoretical possibility that there might not be the necessary two-thirds majority in parliament for allowing an election. It is hard to imagine, however, an Opposition who blocked an election in such circumstances. Nor is an attempt to put together an alternative government, if Johnson has lost a vote of confidence, from disparate elements in the present House of Commons very likely to succeed, though it has been discussed.

More plausible however is a vicious parliamentary battle over whether Parliament could be dissolved before a majority to change the 31 October date could be effective – a version of the pro-rogation debate which has already taken place. If an election was called to pre-empt defeat in a bill to change the default date, then I suppose that the present House might stop the calling of an election until such a bill was passed, meaning that we would remain in the EU while the election was fought. Such a bill would, I think, have to go the whole hog of withdrawing article 50, since this is an option open to unilateral action by the British parliament, while the request for a further extension to the leaving date is not since it has to be agreed by Europe. Such a request would anyway have to come from the government and not from parliament. The likelihood of a Johnson government asking the EU for an extension while an election was fought seems vanishingly small. Far more likely, Johnson would ask the Queen for a dissolution which cannot be refused, and during which he would remain Prime Minister. And perhaps he would set the date for the election to run over 31 October.

The Government, as of when I write, makes it clear that its intention is to leave with a renegotiated deal by 31 October. Failing that, it intends to call an election *after* we have left with no deal, assuming it will be rewarded for achieving Brexit, and trying to fight on that one issue alone: 'We kept the faith'. Although it is not impossible that they will be forced one way or another into an election before we have left, because parliament in some way has prevented no deal and altered the 31 October date. In that case, Johnson would be fighting on an even more immediate demand to be backed for no-deal Brexit, 'Give me a Parliament which will allow me to take us out, whatever it costs!'

Now, it is famously difficult to concentrate the mind of the electorate on one single issue in a General Election, but on this occasion, it might be done. Who knows in the summer of 2019 who would win such an for having done so. Assume he squeezes the Brexit party vote and wins. The victory would not be a normal Conservative victory. The House would contain within its majority a collection of MPs of a variety of political views and hues all on issues other than Brexit – the majority with Conservative labels, some with Brexit Party labels, a few with Labour or Independent Labour labels, some from the DUP. They might have the votes to insist on Brexit at any price, or they might have, as it were, received the reward for having achieved such a thing, but they would find it impossible to build a coherent policy on what to do next. Some would be Socialism-in-one-country Bennites, others antique nostalgic British imperialists. Some would be red in tooth and claw Singapore-on-Thames low tax, low regulation free-traders (Singapore is in fact not at all like that, but never mind.) Some would think global warming a myth, like Lord Lawson; others would see Britain alone as a City on the Hill to lead the world towards a carbon free future (like the Prime Minister's father). Others would be protectionist nationalists on the model of President Trump. And so on and so forth.

They would face an almost equally disparate minority in such a parliament, made up of Conservative Remainers, including perhaps a few in Scotland, some Labour, (I am assuming Labour had been damaged by an election which would have seen either Conservatives or the Brexit party take a good many of their seats) and probably a large number of Liberal Democrats, taking seats both from Labour and from the Conservatives in the south, and there would of course be the SNP, probably in even greater numbers.

Neither side of the House would be able to form a government with any agreed programme on any subject other than the furtherance or prevention of Brexit-at-any-cost, or (depending on the timing of the election) the acceptance of congratulations or obloquy for its achievement. Most particularly, the Hard-Brexiteers themselves, made up of members from a range of prosperous Conservative seats, working class 'left behind' seats perhaps won in such an election either by the Conservatives themselves, or by the Brexit party or by breakaway Labour candidates and the DUP, would find it immediately impossible to create a programme as to what to do about Brexit once achieved, let alone anything else, which satisfied the interests of candidates united only in a mandate to 'get us out'.

The minority side of the House might do a little better in terms of unity – there is perhaps more in common between the leadership and the voters of Remain Conservatives, Liberal Democrats, and Remain Labour – but they would have fought on a ticket of stopping

Brexit, and lost. How on earth could they turn such a defeat into coherent programme for a future government any more than the triumphant Leavers? It would be ridiculous for such a disparate opposition immediately to start campaigning to reverse Brexit, as the Liberal Democrats presently say they will do. A Britain which has left the EU would only be able to rejoin on far different terms than our present membership: we would need to join the Euro, we would lose all John Major's hard-won exemptions (from the Schengen free travel area, for example) and we would lose Mrs Thatcher's famous rebate. There would also need to be another referendum.

The task of persuading the British to rejoin on such terms any time soon would be impossible, I would judge. What is more, there might be modern de Gaulles in Europe who would conclude that to readmit this most troublesome of members would not be in the interest of the European project in any case. And who could blame them? For a different Britain, and in a relatively distant future things might be different, as I shall argue below, but that narrative is of no relevance to next year or the year after.

Thus, *either* outcome of such a Brexit-only election would be instability. On the one hand, there would be a hard and disruptive Brexit, followed by further instability, both in the country and in Parliament. There would sooner or later have to be yet another election to try to find a stable majority to manage the consequences, including the possibly irresistible pressure for another independence referendum in Scotland and quite possibly Northern Ireland, too. By then the United Kingdom might have been without stable government for years and years and years. Picking up the pieces would be, to put it mildly, a heroic task.

If on the other hand the hard-Brexit Johnson election strategy failed, as well it might, stability would not be restored either. Say the Liberal Democrats did very well, that Labour held many seats on the simple strategy of attacking the Johnsonians as hard right-wingers who had in addition failed to deliver their magical Brexit by 31 October, and that there was a rump of surviving, non-deselected Remainer Conservatives and independents – and the SNP. It is hard to imagine a stable government for business-as-usual derived from such a majority, but more immediately, what would they do about Brexit? It is unlikely that they could unite around anything other than a second referendum. Then we are back in the dangerous territory I have already tried to describe, of the Great Betrayal. What is more, of course, the second referendum might not change anything, another year of conflict and anger would have ensued, and it would be difficult still to see the other side of my sulphurous ditch.

My former colleagues in the Conservative party are hoping for magic; the magic of an orderly Brexit of some sort delivered by this Parliament by 31 October, followed by the victory of a reasonably centrist Conservative government committed to a coherent policy: committed not only for future long-term relations with Europe, but on all the other pressing, business-as-usual but dangerous issues of the day. Eton has produced some magnificent Prime Ministers in its history: Walpole, Chatham, Gladstone, Salisbury, Macmillan. If Johnson pulls off the programme for which the Conservatives of the summer of 2019 are yearning, he will be among the greatest of them all. Otherwise, the company of Anthony Eden awaits.

I cannot predict the next few months, let alone the date by when the ditch will finally have been crossed. However, if I am right that the chaos has much deeper roots than the single referendum on Europe and its chaotic interaction with parliamentary democracy, it lies ultimately in the collapse of the narrative by which the United Kingdom has lived since it was crafted after the Second World War by Attlee, Beveridge and Butler on the domestic front, and by Churchill and Macmillan in relation to our position in the world. Unless we create such long lasting narratives again, there will be no hope of a satisfactory succeeding period of reasonably stable government.

Just at this moment I cannot clearly see who plays the part of Attlee or of Butler, creating enough consensus around the role of the state domestically; let alone Churchill, who provided the poetry of the Three Circles, and Macmillan who concluded that having disposed of Empire, membership of the Third Circle entailed actual European membership. Perhaps, to the grave irritation of *Guardian* readers, Eton may offer a Rory Stewart or a Jesse Norman. Perhaps more plausibly, the chaos will have at least the beneficent effect of throwing up new visionary leaders from quite new sources. People do emerge, and sometimes from surprising places. But such leaders must have a story to tell, a story which will resonate with enough people to be effective in forging a new sense of national identity around a new national narrative. 'Without vision, the people perish,' says the Book of Proverbs. And so they would, not literally, but in the loss of their sense that they are a people, governable by a democracy which mediates their disagreements, with the institutions of that democracy founded upon enough shared allegiance to allow the institutions to work by consent.

9   Singapore-on-Thames

THIS ESSAY IS NOT a doomed attempt to foretell how we manage to scramble across the toxic ditch of anger and conflict which lies before us, as we either leave the European Union, or do not. As I have argued, if we leave without a deal after endorsement of such a policy by general election, or even by a second referendum, an immense series of issues in relation to trade, security and the shape of the kingdom will face us, all against the background of anger from those who will have lost out in the general disruption.

If the leaving is thwarted, how do we avoid the creation of a betrayal myth? Or if Remainers inherit a country which has left, what do they do next? I think that even before we have fought our way across the ditch, it is not too early to try to sketch some alternative national narratives around which, over time, people might regroup in sufficient numbers to allow us to say that a new national identity has emerged. What we must not do is tell ourselves a new story which will not work in order to replace the old one, which worked but is now broken. Here will be the test for our political wisdom, learnt over Mr Gaitskell's thousand years of history: can we find a plausible new narrative?

Let us try out first the story offered by some Brexiteers. Britain would become a low tax, free-trading, entrepôt nation wholly outside the EU, attracting mobile capital and highly skilled people, and trading where it could increasingly outside the EU single market and customs union, presumably counting on a lower exchange rate to compensate for the tariffs it would face from Europe and from other former trading partners of the EU. Patrick Minford of Cardiff University and Lord Lilley, former Conservative Cabinet Minister, have argued for such a future. Now, for the purposes of this part of my discussion, I am putting aside the disruption that would already have occurred as we arrive on the other side of the ditch somehow. Does such a free-trading, low-taxing 'swashbuckling', 'Singapore-on-Thames' future look like a narrative which works? Napoleon is said to have claimed that the reason Britain fought him so determinedly was to keep down the price of the sugar in their tea, and told us that we were a nation of shop-keepers. Could we in fact become so now?

Some of us might welcome it. Ironically, the part of England that voted most firmly for Remain, the cosmopolitan, multiracial enterprise and cultural hub of London and its satellites, might do quite well. Though it is impossible to imagine (I am glad to say) that great city ever achieving the level of somewhat sinister self-discipline to be found in Singapore, it is not impossible to imagine London's prosperity continuing under such a scenario. The financial centre would be quite severely damaged if its free access to Europe was curtailed, as it would be. The Eurozone would be bound to reclaim a major part of its own financial transactions, but the City could probably rebuild in other directions. True, it would be the first time that London as a financial centre had ever operated without a formal multinational hinterland, either of Empire and sterling area, or of Europe behind it, but something formidable would plausibly regenerate. Perhaps this is why so many of my very richest financier friends seem to be Brexiteers or not to care one way or the other; their businesses are not much concerned with ordinary financial transactions of the European economy as such.

Similarly, the newest parts of the entrepreneurial world might continue to thrive, if the culture of England was sufficiently supportive in education, tax, science and crucially, freedom of movement for skilled and not-so-skilled labour. (Of course, I am not here discussing the transition to this post-EU world during which all sorts of existing, more traditional industries, from sheep farming to motor manufacturing would surely have suffered, and in which existing networks in for example scientific cooperation would have been damaged.)

Again, the irony is that these enterprises, often younger in both senses of the word, have very often been led by people who voted Remain. Their very enterprise would most likely see them through – if they felt anchored here enough by a supportive culture and did not simply move, as it is easy for them to do. Berlin, for example, is a rapidly-growing entrepreneurial and cultural hub and there is always America. Such businesses would probably become more footloose as they became bigger: rather as James Dyson, Brexiteer and successful world-wide exporter, has become rather footloose. Perhaps fear of a Corbyn Government had something to do with that.

Or, to put it another way, unless the 'swashbuckling' culture was so firmly-rooted that, like Singapore's, it never really faced the challenge of political change (never faced the threat of a Corbyn, for example) such free spirits might be rather unstable long-term participants in the new Britain. Singapore's solution has been to prioritise wealth over true democracy. Its governance, though on the whole civilised, is more like that of the Venetian Republic, opaque, oligarchical, and stable. No risk of Corbyn there, but such a culture would be exceedingly difficult to install in any nation of our size, where, thank goodness, there will always be too many whose genes carry political DNA like that of the anarchic Bristolian protestors of 1831. So perhaps vigorous free enterprise, and ironically mostly Remain-voting entrepreneurs might thrive in such a Britain. I do not, incidentally, mean just business entrepreneurs; radical freedom can produce the explosions of creativity in all fields which ancient Athens, Queen Anne's England, or Weimar Germany unloosed.

However there are difficulties, familiar through history, in maintaining a national narrative solely on the foundation of radical freedom, for business people or creative artists. On what do the rules of civil society rest which prevent such a society become wholly anarchic, in which the strongest, richest, most able and most articulate alone thrive? The market needs rules which cannot be derived from the market. As Keith Thomas argues in his *In Pursuit of Civility*, the rules needed to make it possible to live together, based on slow-grown habits as well as the evolution of rules embodied in law, do not just appear by magic and are quite easily eroded by anarchy, even if for a time the anarchy is pleasantly creative. It has always been the paradox of liberalism (in the proper sense) that it is parasitic upon non-liberal rules without which it soon descends into anarchy.

Now the real Singapore, as opposed to the imaginary Singapore of the swashbucklers' dreams has in fact rested itself on extremely strict rules, both of behaviour and law, derived from ancient Chinese practice, embodied by the founding family, and strictly enforced. It seems very implausible that Britain could dash for individualistic freedoms on the one hand, while returning to a consensus around social conservatism at the same time.

Britain is not a small city state, built from the near tabula rasa of a former British trading post and naval base. We are a nation not of continental scale, but quite big, at the moment of sixty-five million, and growing fast. Those other tens of millions outside the expanding creative hubs are part of the nation too: what of them?

Let us take a step back. There is a natural correlation between those areas which entered the industrial revolution first – Glasgow and its surroundings, Belfast, the northeast of England, which therefore also saw the first decline of industrialisation – and socialism or social democracy. They declined first, in Britain as in many other countries, as other centres elsewhere imitated them and leapfrogged over them. As great industries decline, jobs and communities suffer and whole social and political structures collapse, it is natural for people to turn to government for help. That is perhaps why in the last century (at least once the green/orange religious divide declined, as it will surely also decline too in Northern Ireland in due course) most of the areas of industrial Scotland have normally voted to the left of the kingdom as a whole, and so did large areas of northern England and south Wales.

Why then are these the very areas in Scotland where Scottish nationalism is strongest, and in England where anti-EU feeling is most powerful? I would argue that both responses, though apparently very different in terms of political programmes, derive from common origins. Formerly industrial left-leaning Scotland voted nationalist and therefore pro-European, seeing Europe as a route to express its nationalism. The immediately superior tier of government which received the blame for its discontent was that of the United Kingdom dominated by England and often ruled by Conservatives, seen as having frustrated the desired socialism of industrially declining Scotland.

Similar areas in England, and to some extent Wales, put the blame for their frustrations on *their* immediately superior tier of government; Europe, seen once again as having frustrated their hopes. Since long periods of socialist government had not helped them, these areas turned to a form of nationalism to express their frustration and voted against their respective unions of the UK and of the EU respectively. Far greater courage in the presentation of the benefits of a much older Union saved Scotland for the United Kingdom in its referendum of 2014; timidity about similar arguments for Europe helped, as I have argued, in the loss of the European referendum of 2016.

Now, how does the swashbuckling, Singapore-on-Thames model go down in these areas? The grievances are, perhaps unfairly, against the interventionist institutions which have been called upon to deal with the consequences of industrial and economic decline. Due to the inherent difficulty of any institution, however socially democratic, stopping such decline, people seek someone to blame for the failure. So Leavers they become (of one union or the other) blaming 'remote Westminster' or 'remote Brussels'. To put it mildly, the dose of radical free market or cultural individualism offered by the swashbucklers seems unlikely to strike much of a chord in such regions. In so far as such a doctrine has a name in such places, it is Thatcherism, and that is not a banner under which to rally many hearts and minds in Glasgow, Sunderland, or the valleys of south Wales.

Nevertheless, the swashbucklers have a story to offer. I do not myself think it is one around which we are likely to rally as a nation. Much as I respect his contrarian voice, Patrick Minford is unlikely, I think, to be the author of our new national narrative. If English politicians were brave enough to go down that route, I think they would fail, and most likely lose Scotland and Northern Ireland from our union into the bargain.

10 The USAGBNI?

SOME BREXITEERS SKETCH OUT our future not as
Singapore-on-Thames, but as a sort of adjunct to America. They argue that we should replace our relationship
with Europe with a closer relationship with the USA even
than that imagined by the so-called Special Relationship.
We would have one circle only: the American. It would
start with a bilateral free trade agreement, perhaps involving Britain's joining the somewhat troubled North
Atlantic Free Trade Area which has been the subject of
much criticism by President Trump, or by some bilateral
agreement. And perhaps it might go even further.

This is perhaps a special case of the 'Singapore-on-
Thames' idea. In this case we adopt the economic and
social culture of America rather than that invented by
Lee Kuan Yew. It is often proposed by people who believe that trading with America is a straightforward option. Most experience belies this – American companies

are exceedingly powerful. American legislators normally and understandably put America first, and always have done. In sensitive areas such as the environment and agriculture and healthcare and defence, Britain's culture has been, and is likely to remain, rather different from that of the USA. More fundamentally, it would seem odd to object to rule-taking from the EU, where we are one of the three largest national players involved in formulating those rules, in order to accept rule-taking from an immense partner such as America which has been known, like all hegemonic powers, to trample on smaller animals.

Such a partnership would either be rather marginal, if it excluded many areas where pressure groups on both sides would allow little movement, or, for Britain, exceedingly risky, if our pressure groups were overridden and the power of American interests replaced those of Germany and France. German and French interests, where they conflict with ours, are at least mediated by European institutions where we are players of equal weight and can sometimes win. We may get run over by the German carmakers or French agriculturalists, but Frankfurt and Paris complain just as loudly about the dominance of London in finance.

I include this dream of a new kind of Special Relationship for completeness rather than as a likely option, since the congressional and parliamentary difficulties in the way of any bilateral deal of real significance seem very great. And I do not take it that even the most devoted British lovers of the United States (among whose number I would in many ways count myself) is proposing to swap our membership of the EU for the full blooded and logical end state of such thinking: membership of the United States as three or four new states. A USAGBNI would be rather fun to design (would they accept a restored monarchy? What would the flag look like? What about the Fourth of July? Would Welsh become an official language of the Senate? Would they learn to play cricket again as they did in the eighteenth century?)

Perhaps something along these lines had happened in the prequel to Orwell's *1984* which had landed Britain with the new name of Airstrip One.

But the parlour game is worth playing, if only to remind ourselves that too close an attachment to a superpower, whether American or European, without any control of that power's behaviour, is a strategy like that of the young Lady of Riga, who rode on the back of a tiger. And after all, was it not alarm about the end point of such journeys that led the hard line Brexiteers to vote against Mrs May's proposed close deal with the EU in the first place?

11   The Return

LET US LOOK FOR a moment, at a narrative at the other extreme: the Remainers at all costs. Or, depending on the electoral roulette wheel of the next twelve months, what we might call the 'Rejoiners'. For the purpose of my argument, it does not much matter whether they have been part of an alliance which has won a general election and presumably a subsequent second referendum for Remain, or have lost and started campaigning immediately, as Matthew Parris urges they should, to rejoin the EU. Is there a national narrative for full blown, whole-hearted participation in the European federal project? For starting all over again?

The story would be rather like that which caught my imagination briefly as a teenager and student. It would go something like this. The day of the national state as the most effective protector and centre of allegiance for citizens is past. Just as once the Scots and

Welshmen (but, thanks to religion, racial prejudice and incompetence on the part of the British, not the majority of the Irish) subsumed their allegiance to their own nationhood into that of the United Kingdom, so now all of us should do the same into that of Europe. The Scots and the Welsh did it to gain economic advantage, but also because their and England's interests were very similar. They all shared in the benefits of Empire, and all benefited from well-founded institutions which balanced liberty and solidarity effectively, mediated clashing interests, and delivered internal peace and prosperity. Border wars faded from memory to become the subjects of romances by Sir Walter Scott; tribal conflict became the songs sung at Cardiff Arms Park.

So well did the pooled allegiance work that all (including the Irish) fought with extraordinary valour in the interests of the United Kingdom. All, except the Irish, at one time or another, provided a ruling dynasty for the Kingdom. When facing the rival interests of Germany, the United States, France, China or Japan a hundred years ago this United Kingdom made all citizens members of an entity of a scale that could face any enemy. Intense local loyalties did not dissolve, nor were local cultures diminished, but a British entity created the extraordinary allegiance which fought at Minden and at Trafalgar and Waterloo, on the Somme and in Normandy and the jungles of Burma.

Now is the time, the argument would continue, going slowly and taking even more care to protect local loyalties, to advance this process onto the European scale. Imagine as I once did, the mighty nation of Europe, with its provincial cities of London, Paris, Rome, Berlin, Prague, Budapest, Warsaw and all the rest; rooted in Judaeo-Christianity and the civilisation of ancient Greece, but renewed now by what we should accept as the beneficent legacy of its former imperialism, namely the admixture into European culture of Islamic, African, Indian and other traditions too. Such an entity, facing up to continental powers such as the America, India, China, and rising Africa could protect its citizens where protection is necessary, and cooperate with other great powers where cooperation is vital, such as on the planetary issues of climate change, disease, the regulation of immense global corporations, and the spread of weapons of mass destruction.

Leading by example, like New Zealand or Canada is attractive, but when you have to face down global corporations, rescue your citizens from Iranian or Chinese prisons, or agree on effective measures of climate control, the power wielded by your membership of a great bloc will always be of a different scale than that which you can wield on your own, as a sixty or seventy million, medium-sized nation. The latter will always be a rule taker with little voice in *the formulation of the rules.* So, go for it, but not apologetically: join the currency, push for the absolutely necessary fiscal unity which must go with the single currency, help to design real democratic institutions to govern that fiscal entity, press hard for European defence forces and intelligence services of the quality we are used to and accept that America cannot be expected to defend us, though shared interests in liberal democracy are likely always to make us allies. The Russians and Chinese will probably not welcome another strong player. Nor indeed will many in in America. If Putin and Trump are against you, surely it is evidence that you are doing the right thing, in your interest not theirs? Take back control – of the Europe of which we are a part, for Europeans. Become one of the leaders pushing for the dissolution of nationalities in Europe, and the creation of a true European identity.

I believe that story could be made into one which resounds in the British Isles at least as loudly as anywhere else in Europe. Indeed, because it would give the best chance of preventing the likely break up of our own subsidiary Union, it might be fought for by strong voices throughout the kingdom, and would serve best to help heal our relations with Ireland, as even its half-hearted, Sir Humphrey version has already helped to do as the background to the Good Friday Agreement.

Returnism would of course depend completely on what happened next in Europe. If some of John Gray's darker predictions about the future of the EU came about, (Gray, *op. cit.*) with the failure to respond to its people's demands leading ultimately to disintegration, then there would be nothing of value to rejoin. Our own rebuilt institutions might well feel, and be, safer. Returnism would depend on real leadership in Europe creating a democratically-governed federal entity with efficient government at home and the power to defend its citizens abroad. Such success is far from a foregone conclusion and some of Britain's genuine friends in Europe fear that our departure lessens the chances of its achievement.

If Brexit had happened, then the difficulties for the success of Returnism in the immediately foreseeable future are obvious and immense. I set them out earlier. Our own institutions had not lost our allegiance as those in Europe after the Second World War (Jean Monnet, co-founder of the European institutions is alleged to have said that Britain's problem was that she had won the war). England at least is a very ancient political entity, much older than that of Germany, Italy,

Spain or France in terms of anything like their present borders, as Robert Tombs shows. Our own union has worked very well (except in Ireland). Persuading people openly to consign these to the past is a truly heroic challenge and would be even more heroic if we had not long before passed through a horrible passage of time actually leaving the Europe we now proposed to rejoin.

But two new arguments which could be deployed in favour of a new full-hearted application to Europe would have been added before such a campaign started in earnest. The very process of extricating ourselves, or attempting to extricate ourselves, from the EU and the shatteringly divisive experience of clambering across what I have called the sulphurous and toxic ditch of Brexit, the worst of it still to come, will have itself damaged the institutions which had indeed served us so well. The British constitution already looks sick, and will look sicker still before we are done with Brexit. Few doubt that radical constitutional surgery will be needed in Britain, whatever happens. Why not then the radical step of rebuilding our forms of government within the European project, making a renewed application for membership an explicitly constitutional programme, as it arguably should always have been?

Second, the genuine danger of generating a betrayal myth would have been put to rest because in this first scenario, Brexit is not halted but completed, and found to be the beginning not of a brave new world but of debilitating mediocrity. We would be rewinding history to the 1960s and taking the European step again, but in a quite different manner: head on and honestly.

There is, however, a second scenario where the full-blooded European commitment of what I have called Returnism would, paradoxically, also be required. Imagine a situation where, after the turmoil of the next twelve months or so, and perhaps a second referendum won for Remain, we found ourselves still in membership of the EU. Proponents of the betrayal myth would be in full voice. The nation would find itself in an uncomfortable status quo ante: to the relief of many in business we would still be in possession of our privileged of membership of the EU, outside the Eurozone, inside most of the rest, but our domestic politics would be in complete confusion. Nigel Farage or his successors would be on the campaign trail once again, to reverse now 'the Betrayal' and take us towards another attempt at Brexit. We might at last have some violence on the streets. Now consider what kind of Remainism would be needed in the face of such a second onslaught. Would the only hope then for Remainers not be to fight as full-bloodedly as their opponents? Openly to espouse a new patriotism for Europe? Not take the Sir Humphry line, but finally go full tilt for the real deal?

Surely it would beggar belief after all the damage done to our relations with the other members that we could attempt to argue that we should continue, semi-detached as if nothing had happened? Surely if we remained we would have to become full-blooded members at last – or run the risk of going around the whole dreadful circuit all over again?

A return to what I have called the Sir Humphrey style of membership, grudgingly belonging and applying the brake to every attempt at ever closer union, must be the worst approach to our future of all. We simply could not continue with a narrative telling us that the EU was only an economic entity; we would laugh ourselves out of court. We would have been embroiled in the painful process of the destruction of our old Three Circles myth since 2016. No one could hope to persuade us anymore that we were happy half-in, half-out, exceptionalist in our geopolitics and unique among EU members in our separation from the central political drive of Europe.

Even if we somehow find ourselves still in Europe on the other side of the Brexit ditch, with the ruins of our national institutions all around us and cries of betrayal echoing in the streets – *even then*, perhaps *especially* then, we will need a new narrative, and the new narrative from the Remainers would have to be full-blown commitment to Europe. Heraclitus said, you cannot step into the same river twice. We could not recreate the old narrative that said we had half-committed ourselves to Europe after the bitter turmoil of the Brexit conflict. We would have to decide. Thanks to Margaret Thatcher, John Major and Gordon Brown, and to the considerable patience of our European colleague nations, we had won for ourselves a privileged position of semi-membership. We then chose to throw that fragile status away. We must face the fact that it has been smashed forever by the truth-telling political savagery of Brexit. We must face the fact that if we stay after all this, we must stay as full members with all that entails.

Once returned to membership, or rather committed for the first time to real membership rather than the Sir Humphrey version, we would bid fond farewell to the poetry of the Three Circles (while of course hoping as Europeans to maintain good relationships based on equality with America, and with the Commonwealth's rising behemoths of India and Africa). Our national narrative would now be that of Europe. My children and grandchildren, multi-ethnic and multinational as they happen to be, would all be securely European, and

12 Punching at our Correct Weight

THERE IS A FOURTH narrative to offer. If swashbuckling does not work, joining America is not really an option and a full-blooded reversal of Brexit and true commitment to Europe is too heroic, is there a fourth way?

Imagine us having crossed the ditch. In the process of crossing, all our institutions are damaged in the way I fear but of course life goes on. The world has not stopped circling the sun, which still rises every day. The economy, damaged for a time, readjusts, not by heroic free-trading and the creation of an enormous entrepot economy, but by slowly rebuilding new connections, some in Europe, some not. We are undoubtedly poorer than we otherwise would have been, but we slowly revert to trend growth rates, with a weaker currency mediating our new economic relationship with the world.

As before, we remain a bourgeois country, with a large middle class, a relatively high standard of living, and very widespread ownership of property. We are very unfertile ground for Marxist experiments of the Corbyn or McDonnell type, but we are also used to a high level of social solidarity built on the institutions of the welfare state. No one is going to get many votes by dismantling them, however much they may swash their buckle.

But the welfare state is expensive and will get more expensive. We have, in this scenario, left the European Union. Let us assume for a moment what I do not in my heart believe, that we can leave Europe without losing Scotland and risking Northern Ireland, too: but say we are the same old kingdom, on our own, a bit poorer for the time being and returning with great vehemence to what I have called the business-as-usual politics of health, social care, education, inequality, law and order, infrastructure and so forth – all against the implacable background of the growing pressures of climate change. We will need to repair damaged institutions which failed to mediate successfully between the demands of Leavers and Remainers. Political parties will need to be reformed and rebuilt as the temporary alliances of Leave versus Remain become irrelevant.

A constitutional settlement will be needed to see that the ill-considered head-on collision between referendum politics and parliamentary politics does not happen again, with a written set of rules defining what our constitution is, and how we change it; when a referendum should be used, and how parliament should handle the consequences. I am sure in the ensuing work our bicameral parliament and probably our voting system would be radically reformed. We would need, as a fully autonomous nation, to decide how to entrench those parts of our constitution which needed it but which could not plausibly after all this rest on unwritten conventions. We would need to decide on our future relationship to the European Convention on Human Rights, but we would need to consider much more than that.

If we were to remain a state that could pay for the necessary welfare, we could not, I think, hope to pretend that we had a defence establishment left over from the days when we were, at least at first, the second military power in the NATO alliance. Attlee wanted a British atomic bomb so that we could be at the 'top table' and because the McMahon Act of 1946 cut Britain out of the nuclear partnership to which we, along with Canada, had given so much help during the wartime Manhattan Project – another example of 'America first' in action. Brown and Cameron wanted aircraft carriers so that we could sail the seven seas alongside the US Navy. Many in the Conservative party who may not be entranced with Singapore-on-Thames, hope for a sort of mini superpower Britain post-Brexit, with allies no doubt, but global in our own right. This, I believe, is another fantasy.

What we surely would be – and should be happy to be – is something rather different: a larger Canada offshore from Europe, living in a civilised way with our own traditions of culture, science and the rest properly funded. This, with proper investment in our economic and social infrastructure and no pretensions to exceptional status. Would such a nation really be sensible to pay for aircraft carriers and state of the art nuclear ballistic submarines, with all that goes with making both work? Should we not respectfully be saying 'farewell' to such trappings of great powerdom which have derived from our past Three Circles national narrative, and perhaps indeed have their origins far back in our period as a real superpower?

Certainly, we should need alliances; certainly we should deploy serious money on making ourselves the hardest of possible targets for terrorist attack and organised crime – including maintaining our spend on first rate security services and investing in rather nearer to first-rate police. There is plenty to do on the home front to keep our citizens safe, not much of it helped by the deployment of aircraft carriers. We have not really yet begun, for example, to tackle the importation, along with all that joyous diversity, of the less joyous multinational criminal gangs (to which our home-grown variety can add their own traditions). Nor are we yet the world leaders we sometimes claim to be in cyber defence, nor do we have adequate border patrols or protection for the fisheries we would have reclaimed post-Brexit (if we can find ways of continuing to sell our catches to the Spanish and French who actually eat them).

Considering security in a wider sense, we have not yet settled down to tackle the divisions in our society which derive from the arrival of quite large communities who, as yet, show no real intention of abandoning the traditions of their homelands. Traditions which sometimes seriously conflict with what we regard and do not intend to give up regarding, as civilised behaviour: the eradication of FGM and the acceptance as normal of LGBT+ fellow-citizens come to mind. We are not about to go back on compromises hammered out between Christianity and secularism in the last century even to be welcoming to new arrivals, fundamentalist Christian, Muslim, or of any other faith or belief system. Such issues take time and care and often, money, to mediate. Only by building national community can we hope to dissolve these sometimes difficult subsidiary communities. But the new national community has genuinely to adapt where it can without compromising fundamental values to the new arrivals. A new narrative, freed of post-imperial decoration is essential to this task too.

And there is plenty more to do. We have enormous disparities not just in wealth, which may within reason be tolerated as inevitable in a free society, but in health and education, which are not. Should we not be focussing on these issues – business-as-usual I have called them, but massively important unfinished business-as-usual – as the way of rebuilding trust in institutions? We would need, on our own, to be decarbonising our economy (and not just by moving carbon-rich industry off shore). We would need to be prepared for pandemics, and considering the power to harm as well as to help of artificial intelligence. These are all tasks for which our scientific and engineering ingenuity fit us rather well. Looking after ourselves we would of course join any international action which looked effective. But we could not do all this while playing at being an autonomous policeman for the world, even as sidekick to an American or European sheriff.

Such a narrative, again, would need great skill in the telling. We are obsessed with our heroic military past: never a year goes by without the remembrance of some great defeat or victory of long ago. As I write, well-meaning people are writing to the papers saying that we need a navy which should be able to police the Persian Gulf by itself, protect mostly foreign owned British flagged vessels wherever they may be threatened on the high seas, stand up to the Russians, rescue ill-treated citizens in foreign jails, defend protestors in Hong Kong from bullying by Beijing and generally, in that much-used phrase, punch above our weight around the world. Would it not really be a better strategy to punch *at* our weight? Most boxers do. Ah, but we are members of the Security Council of the UN!

Nothing could bring more sharply into focus what this fourth narrative should entail than that it should involve our surrender of that Security Council place, given to us when we were indeed one of the superpowers of the world. Give it up! Get real! Be a medium-sized, wealthy, well-run modern nation, a centre of civilised living and a participant in every sensible alliance aimed, for example, at climate control, or mutual European defence. Do not let us drive ourselves mad by trying to play at continental games when we are a nation with the same population as one province of India, China, or Indonesia, and an economic heft comparable to one big state of the USA or the EU!

We would need leaders with the genius of Kemal Attaturk to reformulate our position in the world and modernise it, so that reality and our national narrative coincided in the way that he led Turkey's to do after the dissolution of the Ottoman Empire. His task was easier – the Ottoman Empire had suffered catastrophic defeat. For Turkey a new narrative *had* to be found. However this fourth story, which is in reality the best and safest story because it needs the least bending of the truth, is in the present climate the least easy for which to find champions. The Leavers are too much imbued with slightly comic imperial nostalgia (please, no more fighting the executives of BMW on the beaches of Normandy). After we leave, according to them, we are going to spend far more, not as in my scenario less, on defence (as well as on everything else). Such a narrative, based on nostalgia and not reality would be desperately dangerous, as ending in another collision between reality and our national self-identity, with yet further postponement of the necessary rebuilding of institutions based on the truth.

On the other hand, Remainers are doing little better. They seem to think they can stop the nightmare and simply wake up where we were before ('bollocks to Brexit' is not a very comprehensive strategy for national identity.) There are not very many willing to look in a clear-eyed way at a future where Britain, after a time of painful transition, will be for the first time since the first Elizabeth's day, an 'empire' in the sense that the queen understood the word. That is, a nation accountable to no one else; free of empire in the later sense; relying on our own, necessarily reformed institutions and discarding the last remnants of a super-power status which has long been incongruous and would then be ridiculous. We could become a pragmatic, prosperous, middle-ranking nation, much more like Canada or Australia than America or China or the unifying EU, but a good place to live and work.

Of course, if we could agree to shed nostalgia and find the comfort of living with a realistic appreciation of our place in the world, the old left/right politics would soon, thank goodness, reappear. There would still be never-ending argument about where to find the correct balance between state versus private enterprise, between freedom and solidarity, and between the attractions and the dangers of trying to build New Jerusalems in this world. Irritatingly, we would find that having left the EU, the amount of irksome bureaucratic regulation would probably go up, rather than down, because there is no nation on earth more prone to the disease of bureaucratic regulation, nor more open to the bullying of single issue pressure groups which generate regulation, than Britain. (India is a possible competitor, but then we taught them how to do it). Whom would we blame for our straight bananas or our non-mailable kippers post Brexit? We would have to go back to the 1950s and dig out that terrifying figure, The Gentleman from Whitehall who Knows Best. He would now be even more terrifying because he would not be a gentleman only. His successor would not be gendered and would be armed with drones and data mining to check that we had put our rubbish in the right recycling bin.

Normal politics would not stop, it would be re-born, but shorn of some of the self-delusion which, I have argued, was necessary to the period of our retreat from imperial superpowerdom but is now pernicious, and is anyway dead and gone.

One further sad outcome might forcefully compel us this way. If through the in-fighting involved in the crossing of the Brexit ditch we have managed to lose from our United Kingdom Scotland as we once lost most of Ireland (and perhaps we would have lost the remainder of Ireland this time too) then the remaining smaller kingdom of England and Wales would not have a choice: our place in the world would have changed so radically that even the most nostalgic of our rulers would surely have noticed that we needed to enter a lower division in the international boxing competition.

For England alone that Security Council seat, bolstered by 'top table' nuclear-armed submarines based where? Plymouth? – would look very odd indeed.

I personally, passionately hope that such a break-up does not happen, not so much because of the undoubted extra weight in the world given to us all in the kingdom by the present Union, but because I think England without Scotland would run the risk of an even worse bout of the disease of English nationalism than has so far emerged around the Brexit debate. The descent from patriotism to an unattractive nationalism – a distinction well made by Orwell – in Scotland at the time of the independence referendum of 2014 was marked. That unattractive descent would, I suspect, be more than matched in England if a second such referendum were to succeed and see Scotland leave.

Our union has been so successful for so long that its destruction would be an even more tragic outcome than a bitter Brexit. As a proud Englishman, I do not want to be left alone with the English. But truly depressing opinion polls tell us that there are some who will swallow even that sad outcome if it is the cost of full independence from Europe for England.

The purpose of this chapter has been to propose that the England they would inherit in such a scenario would not be the England after which many, at least on the right, seem to hanker. It could hold a civilised but middle-ranking place, often probably rather left-leaning (but far from Marxist, with its massive middle class and its respect for moderation) getting to grips with a pragmatic agenda of the emerging social problems of the day. It does not deploy many aircraft carriers, nor send warships to intimidate China. It is not the heroic Britain of 1940 standing alone, because Britain did not stand alone in 1940. As the great cartoonist, Fougasse, had one Tommy say to another, sitting on the white cliffs of Dover looking out to sea in July 1940, 'So our poor old Empire is alone in the world.' 'Aye, we are – the whole five hundred million of us.' (Fougasse, *Running Commentary*, 1941.) If it is clear-eyed about its place in the world, it could be a fine place to live nonetheless. The Brexit party (whether the official party or the Conservative party in disguise) would have disappeared overnight, its single task achieved, as John Gray has pointed out (BBC 4, *A Point of View* 19 July 2019). We would need a new Conservative party, competent to deal with this rather more modest national narrative, run by people much more like R.A. Butler, Kenneth Clarke, and Chris Patten, than the government I see in power as I write in August 2019. It would also need a new Labour party (if Mr Corbyn and Mr McDonnell had not by then succeeded in getting Labour replaced by a resurgent Liberal party) led by people like Alan Johnson, and Hilary Benn and the wicked Blairites – heirs of Attlee and Bevin.

13 Envoi

I HAVE OFFERED FOUR narratives of the kind which we will need to consider once the Brexit ditch is crossed. My belief is that there can be no return to a status quo. We will be living in a different kind of country, one way or another. We will need to choose what kind of country we want. I do not myself consider that the first option I offered, Singapore-on-Thames, is plausible, but others will disagree.

I may be wrong, but full-blooded attachment to America does not look very plausible either.

What I have called 'Returnism' makes sense and may, depending on whether or not the European Union develops successfully, one day grow in attraction. Perhaps most controversially, I believe that if, when the toxic politics of the Brexit ditch is crossed, we were to find ourselves still in Europe, as is just possible, there will be no hope of maintaining our previous status quo of half-membership. We should put aside our doubts and join the enterprise of ever-closer union fully. Otherwise we will be condemned to repeat the political horrors of the last few years, and the next few too, indefinitely.

My fourth way – that of accepting, after a completed Brexit – a middling world significance, concentrating primarily on our own affairs, abandoning the pretence of exceptionalism in our geopolitics, seems the most satisfactory to me. It is not, of course, incompatible with returning one day to Europe on a-full blooded basis. In fact, it might be seen as a necessary step in that direction, slow though the turn that way might be.

Relieved of the effort of carrying the baggage of the remains of our post-imperial past, and of the heavy burden of 'punching above our weight' required by the Three Circles doctrine that was so helpful in its day, we might find that our capacity to address the ever-present business-as-usual problems of politics was much increased. My fourth way would, I think, promise a greater chance of living at ease with one another again, since reality and the national narrative would more nearly coincide, and the institutions we would rebuild would be rebuilt with a pragmatic and realistic purpose in mind.

Perhaps it is too early to start thinking about future narratives when we are still struggling with crossing the toxic Brexit ditch. Events will shape us, and will shape those who will have to try to tell the new stories. But it is surely as well now to begin to try to sketch out what might work and to be clear-eyed about what surely will not. Together with an attempt to elucidate the causes which led us to where we are, such a first sketch of the kind of country we might want to try to build after this crisis is over has been my purpose in this book.

About the Author

WILLIAM WALDEGRAVE IS CURRENTLY Provost of Eton College. He was one of the original members of Lord Rothschild's Think Tank in the early 1970s. He has served as a Member of Parliament and as Minister of State at the UK Department of the Environment and the Foreign Office. At Cabinet level he was Secretary of State for Health, Chancellor of the Duchy of Lancaster, Minister of Agriculture and Chief Secretary to the Treasury. He is a member of the House of Lords. He was a Kennedy Fellow at Harvard University and is a Fellow of All Souls College Oxford. He is married to Caroline Waldegrave OBE, Director of Leith's School of Food and Wine. They have four children and a dairy farming business in Somerset.